D0700095

CIVIC CENTER

SCIENCE
FOUNDATIONS

Light and Sound

SCIENCE FOUNDATIONS

SCIENCE
FOUNDATIONS

Light and Sound

P. ANDREW KARAM AND BEN P. STEIN

CHELSEA HOUSE
PUBLISHERS
An imprint of Infobase Publishing

Science Foundations: Light and Sound

Copyright © 2011 by Infobase Publishing

Chelsea House
An imprint of Infobase Publishing
132 West 31st Street
New York, NY 10001

Library of Congress Cataloging-in-Publication Data
Karam, P. Andrew.
 Light and sound / P. Andrew Karam and Ben P. Stein.
    p. cm. — (Science foundations)
 Includes bibliographical references and index.
 ISBN 978-1-60413-344-8 (hardcover)
 1. Light—Popular works. 2. Sound—Popular works. I. Stein, Ben P. II. Title.
III. Series.
 QC358.5.K37 2010
 535—dc22   2010015736

Chelsea House books are available at special discounts when purchased in bulk quantities for businesses, associations, institutions, or sales promotions. Please call our Special Sales Department in New York at (212) 967-8800 or (800) 322-8755.

You can find Chelsea House on the World Wide Web at
http://www.chelseahouse.com

Text design by Kerry Casey
Cover design by Takeshi Takahashi
Composition by EJB Publishing Services
Cover printed by Bang Printing, Brainerd, MN
Book printed and bound by Bang Printing, Brainerd, MN
Date printed: October 2010
Printed in the United States of America

10 9 8 7 6 5 4 3 2 1

Contents

What Waves Are

The universe began with a burst of light—on this fact, both scientists and many religious leaders agree. Since the universe's birth, it has been permeated by **photons**—particles of light. Some of them are visible to human eyes, but most of them are invisible. The universe radiates photons in a spectrum from low-energy radio waves to high-energy gamma rays, with visible light somewhere in between. The early universe also rang like a very low-pitched bell, and astronomers are only now beginning to learn how to study these cosmic sounds and use them to learn more about the earliest moments of creation.

Sound and **light** are part of everyday life. People gather most of their information about their surroundings through the light that enters their eyes and the sounds that enter their ears. They see reflections in a mirror, the faces of loved ones, and rainbows after a storm. They hear music, voices, and the din of traffic. People put sound to work, too: They use ultrasound to peer inside the body, as well as to clean teeth and jewelry, while elephants and whales use low-frequency sound (infrasound) to communicate over long distances. In addition, the whole science of seismology—the study of earthquakes and the waves that travel through the Earth—depends on the transmission of sound to help reveal the makeup of our planet and the other planets in the solar system. Meanwhile, the field of **helioseismology** helps to reveal the inner workings of the Sun (and is now beginning to be used to study other stars as well). The science of sound, known as **acoustics**, is incredibly valuable on many levels.

Light is even more versatile. In addition to helping us to see, light is also used as a tool in lasers, holograms, fiber optics, and more. If we expand what we consider "light" to include the entire electromagnetic spectrum—from radio and radar waves through X-rays and gamma rays—then light is possibly what reveals the most about the universe.

Both light and sound can first be understood by comparing them to water waves. And so, we will begin this exploration by looking at the basic science of waves.

WAVES OF LIGHT, WAVES OF SOUND

Both light and sound are waves. According to the dictionary, a wave is a disturbance that moves through space over time. That is okay as a definition, but what does it really mean? Imagine a lake or pond (or a swimming pool, or even a bathtub) where the water is completely smooth, with not a wave to be seen. Now, throw in a rock and note how the rock disturbs the water when it hits. Some of the water splashes up in the air and falls back while waves ripple outward from where the rock hit, spreading this disturbance across the water. For another example, think of what happens when you shake a rope at one end—again, the disturbance caused by shaking the rope travels along the rope in the form of a wave.

Sound waves are similar to these sorts of waves: Sound is a disturbance in the molecules of air (or water or other substance) that travels from place to place. Light is a bit different, however, because not only can it travel through "stuff" (air, water, glass), but it can also travel through the **vacuum**, which is empty space. It took centuries before scientists would accept that light could be a wave *and* that space could be empty—they simply could not understand how a wave could travel through nothingness.

Their reaction was understandable because ordinary waves need a **medium**, a substance that waves pass through. Water waves cannot exist without water. Sound does not exist in empty space—sound waves need air or water or something that allows them to travel from one place to another. A wave traveling through a rope needs the rope—otherwise it wouldn't exist.

So, if a wave is a disturbance, how can there be a disturbance when there is nothing to disturb? The answer is that a light wave is an **electromagnetic wave**, and electromagnetic waves don't need a substance to disturb—meaning they can still travel through emptiness. But before we learn more about light, it's time to learn a little more about waves in general.

FUNDAMENTALS OF WAVES: FREQUENCY, AMPLITUDE, AND WAVELENGTH

Waves are made up of different parts, and each one has its own term. Some of these terms will probably be familiar. In fact, the properties of waves are a part of our language, especially when we are talking about radio, radar, and sound.

When we dissect a wave, we find that it has some distinct parts. Begin by drawing a wave on a piece of paper, and then draw a horizontal line through the middle—parts of the wave will rise above the line and parts of it will sink below. The high parts of the wave are called the **crests** and the low parts are called the **troughs** (Figure 1.1). Sometimes they are also called peaks and valleys. Now, make a mark at the very highest part of one peak, and another mark at the highest part of the next peak, and measure the distance between these two marks—this distance is the **wavelength**. The same thing can be seen with the waves at the lake, by the way, and with light waves, waves traveling along a rope, and radio waves. All waves are built the same way: They all have crests, troughs, and wavelengths, and of these features, the most important part of a wave is usually its wavelength.

Amplitude is the term used to describe how tall waves are. The given distance that the wave rises above the reference line is called the amplitude, which can be looked at as a measure of the strength of the wave. For example, the harder a rope is shaken, the higher the peaks and the stronger the amplitude of the wave. It's the same thing with a water wave: Throwing a heavy rock will produce a higher wave (greater amplitude) when compared to a small pebble. In a radio wave, the amplitude is related to the strength of the radio signal.

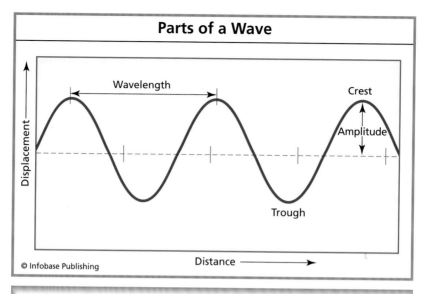

Parts of a Wave

© Infobase Publishing

Figure 1.1 The parts of a wave are the same for radio, radar, and sound waves.

Imagine that your wave moves, so that the crests and troughs travel toward the right side of the page. The **phase** of a wave can tell you the location of the crests and troughs at any given time in relation to where they started. At the beginning, the waves will be exactly where you drew them; a moment later, the crests and troughs will be shifted a little to the right.

Now it's time to talk more about wavelength. Each type of wave moves at a given speed. Light waves, for example, move through the vacuum of space at a speed of about 186,282 miles (299,792,458 meters) per second. Sound waves move much more slowly; through the air at sea level (under specific conditions of atmospheric pressure and temperature), they travel at a speed of about 761 miles (1,225 kilomters) per hour. So, waves can be described in terms of the speed at which they move. And by knowing the wavelength and the speed, it's also possible to calculate the number of wave crests (or troughs) that move past a certain point every second—this is called the **frequency**.

Here is an example of how to calculate the frequency: Say we have a radio wave with a wavelength of about 10 feet (approximately

3 m). Again, this means the distance between the crests of the wave. Radio waves are really an invisible kind of light wave. They travel at the speed of light. Therefore, at this speed, 99.9 million wave crests will pass by every second. The unit of the hertz (abbreviated Hz) denotes when one crest moves by each second, so a radio wave with an approximately 10-foot (3-m) wavelength that is traveling at the speed of light will have a frequency of 99.9 million hertz, or 99.9 megahertz (MHz)—right in the middle of the FM radio band. Of course, it can work the other way, too: If we know the frequency of a radio station, we can calculate the wavelength. Here is the equation for this calculation:

$$f = \frac{v}{\lambda}$$

In this equation, f is the frequency (in hertz), v is the speed of the wave, and λ is the wavelength.

For any radio or light waves, v equals the speed of light (186,282 miles per second [299,792,458 m/s] in a vacuum [empty space]; a little bit slower as it travels through any non-empty space, such as air, water, or glass). The equation below tells us the frequency of the radio waves in the last paragraph:

$$f = \frac{299{,}792{,}458 \text{ m/sec}}{3 \text{ m}} = 99{,}930{,}819 \text{ Hz}$$

This same equation can be used to find the wavelength of any kind of wave with a given frequency as follows:

$$f = \frac{v}{\lambda}, \text{ so } \lambda = \frac{v}{f}, \text{ which gives us } \lambda = \frac{299{,}792{,}458}{99{,}930{,}819} = 3 \text{ m}$$

Using this equation, anyone can calculate the wavelength of their favorite radio station, or of any musical note. For example, middle C on a piano typically has a frequency of about 261 Hz. With a speed of sound of 761 miles per hour (1,225 kilometers per second), a middle C has a wavelength of about 4.3 feet (1.3 m).

WAVES AS A PERIODIC PHENOMENON

Waves—especially sound and light waves—follow a pattern that can be predicted. Think about a cork floating in the water as a series of waves goes by (which were perhaps made by the rock that was thrown in the water in the earlier example). As each wave goes by, the cork will rise up, reach a maximum height, go down as the crest passes, reach a minimum height in the trough, and then start to rise up again. This same process takes place over and over and over again, every time a wave passes by. One way to try to understand the wave is to chart the position of the cork as it rises and falls in response to the waves passing. Charting the cork gives us a sort of graph that shows the shape of the wave. Figure 1.2 shows how the height of the wave (shown on the Y-axis) changes as time passes (shown on the X-axis).

This is what a light wave looks like, too: The crests and troughs pass by like clockwork for as long as the light wave is passing by. A sound wave looks like this, too, with every wave looking just like the one before (as long as nothing happens to change the frequency of the light or the sound). Any phenomenon that regularly repeats the same pattern over and over again is called a **periodic phenomenon**, and light and sound waves are almost perfect examples of periodic phenomena. Water waves are also periodic, but only up to a point because there are too many other factors that can affect them (such as wind, changing water depths, the shoreline, etc.). Therefore, they are not as perfectly periodic as light and sound waves. Perhaps the most important thing that happens to water waves (and most other waves) is that they tend to die out over time; so, a more accurate graph of the cork might actually look more like Figure 1.3.

Anything that repeats regularly like this can be described with mathematics—in this case, by using a branch of math called trigonometry. Although there is no need to understand trigonometry for this book, it is interesting to know that the same types of equations used to describe waves can also be used to describe a bouncing ball, a bouncing spring, a satellite orbiting Earth, the hands of a clock, and anything else that moves in a circle or that moves up and down so regularly.

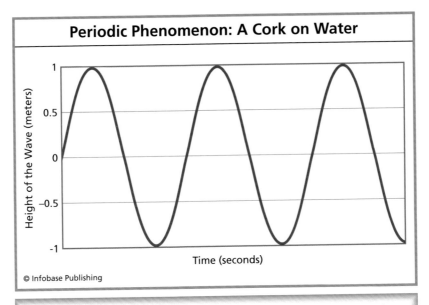

Periodic Phenomenon: A Cork on Water

© Infobase Publishing

Figure 1.2 The height and frequency of a wave is exemplified by this graph, which imagines the movement of a cork floating on water.

TYPES OF WAVES

Take a rubber band, stretch it tight and then pluck it. Chances are that you'll hear a twang or a hum as the rubber band moves back and forth. Every time the rubber band is plucked, it is pushing on the air molecules, pushing them a little closer together and compressing the air. As the rubber band moves in the other direction, the compression stops. In fact, the air becomes a little less compressed. In this case, as a sound wave passes by, we can measure the air pressure and plot it on a graph, ending up with something like the graphs we've already seen. Sound moves through the air as a pressure wave; what we hear as sound is the rapid change in air pressure as the sound wave (the pressure wave) causes our eardrums to vibrate. Sound is a kind of wave known as a **longitudinal wave**—the sound moves in the exact same direction that's parallel to the back-and-forth vibrations of the air molecules.

Now let's think about someone holding a rope down at their side and then shaking their hand back and forth in slow motion.

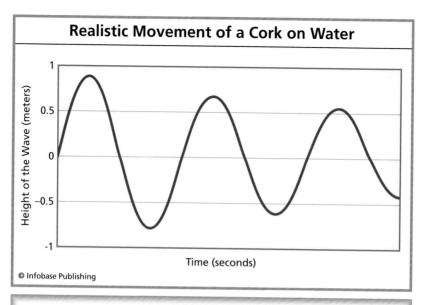

Realistic Movement of a Cork on Water

Height of the Wave (meters)

1

0.5

0

−0.5

-1

Time (seconds)

© Infobase Publishing

Figure 1.3   In reality, waves flatten in time, as shown in this graph.

We would see a wave traveling down the rope: As the hand moves to the right, the rope moves in the same direction. Now, if the person keeps moving their hand to the right, the wave will continue to move to the right, first through the bit of rope closest to the hand, then through the next bit of rope, until it finally reaches the end of the rope—the entire wave is moving to the right. But the crests and troughs of the wave wiggle up and down. This is an example of a **transverse wave**—the wave moves in a direction perpendicular to the up-and-down motion of the wave's crests and troughs.

All the examples given so far are called **traveling waves** because the waves are moving through space. What would happen if the rope were fastened at the other end—perhaps tied to a tree? If the wave moves from left to right to reach the tree, it is reflected back in the other direction, from right to left. If the person keeps on wiggling the rope, then there are waves moving from left to right, and reflected waves from the tree moving right to left. When the waves combine with each other, the combined wave does not seem to move anymore, neither to the right nor to the left. The wave stands in place, forming a series of crests and troughs that just vibrate up and down at the same location. This is called a **standing wave** and it's also what happens when a guitar string is plucked, as it's fastened at both ends.

WAVE EFFECTS: REFRACTION, INTERFERENCE, AND DIFFRACTION

When waves interact with each other, things can get interesting. Visualize what happens when two waves meet: Two sets of crests and troughs pass through each other. When that happens, the waves can reinforce each other, or they can cancel each other out (Figure 1.4A). When two wave crests line up, they reinforce each other and form a combined wave that is larger than either of the two original waves; and when the troughs line up, the resulting trough is much deeper. What is even more interesting is what happens when the crest of one wave lines up with the trough of the other—in this case, the waves cancel each other out and the result is . . . nothing. This is how noise-cancelling headphones work—by analyzing outside sounds and generating the exact opposite wave to cancel out the outside noise. You'll see a different pattern when waves add together (red=wave #1, blue=wave #2, and green=combined waves) (Figure 1.4B).

Waves can also **diffract**, which is to say that they can change direction or spread out as they pass through openings or as they go past a corner. This is why when we call out to someone who is out of sight around a corner, they can still hear us. As the sound waves ripple outward and encounter obstacles, they will bend around them. This happens with all waves—electromagnetic, sound, water, and more. The act of some straight waves passing through a narrow slit is similar to what happens when a person in one room is talking to a person in another room through the door. This not only shows the waves diffracting—spreading out from the slit—but also shows the constructive and destructive interference. Constructive interference is when the waves add to each other to form bigger troughs. Destructive interference is when they cancel each other out.

Diffraction is responsible for the rainbow colors on the back of a CD and DVD. These discs encode their information in narrowly spaced circular tracks, which act as slits. When light hits the disc, the tracks diffract it. When it's ordinary white light that comes from,

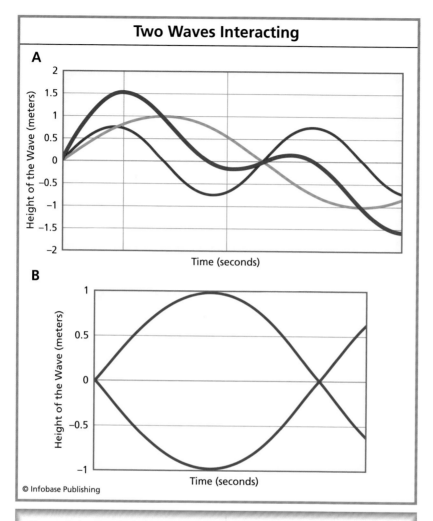

Figure 1.4   Graph A shows what happens when two sets of crests and troughs reinforce each other. Graph B demonstrates how to cancel out a sound wave by wearing noise-canceling headphones. In it, blue=noise, red=the noise-canceling sound wave, and green=the combined wave, in which noise is cancelled out.

say, an overhead lamp, the constructive and destructive interference between the diffracted waves ends up separating the white light into its different rainbow colors.

Yet another phenomenon of waves—one that also happens to any wave—is **refraction**. Refraction refers to the bending that occurs when a wave enters a region where it changes its speed. Imagine a line of people running on a beach toward the water. Instead of aiming to hit the water head-on, the people decide to tilt their line at a 45-degree angle to the water's edge. People who hit the water first will slow down first, and people who hit the water later will slow

Ocean Waves and Tsunamis

Waves can be a deadly force. For example, in 2004, tidal waves off the Indian Ocean killed more than 225,000 men, women, and children.

Normal waves are a lot like any other waves: They transfer energy from one place to another, even though the water itself doesn't travel. Think of the way that a wave travels along a rope; the energy moves from end to end as the rope ripples, but every bit of the rope itself stays in place. Any wave moving through water transfers energy in the same way.

Many water waves are created by wind—light breezes, heavy storms, and everything in between. The difference between small ripples and huge waves reflects the size of the storm. But even the largest wave pales in comparison to a tsunami.

On December 26, 2004, a huge earthquake (with a magnitude of 9.1 to 9.3 on the Richter scale, it is the third-largest ever recorded) jostled the sea floor off the coast of Sumatra, Indonesia. The sudden rise of the seabed displaced a massive amount of water, resulting in a tsunami. The displaced water only made a ripple at the surface of the Indian Ocean, but it was traveling at the speed of an airliner. When the energy from this massive volume of water reached the shores of India, Myanmar, and Thailand, the water piled up into waves that were up to 100 feet (30 m) high. These waves crashed onto the shore and swept away trees, homes, hotels, and people. When the water receded, more than 225,000 people had died in one of the deadliest natural disasters ever recorded.

down later. This change in speed at different times for different people will cause the line to bend toward the water. This is exactly how refraction works—the change in speed causes the bending.

Along the same lines, light does not always move at the same speed. For example, light moves more slowly in water than it does in air. So, when a beam of light travels from air into water, it slows down. This is the reason that a piece of wood or a fishing pole sticking into the water looks as though it is bending.

What Light Is and How It Can Be Used

We spend our lives immersed in light, mainly because we depend on light to see the world around us. Even at night, we can see by moonlight and starlight (though not nearly as well); very few places where people are found on Earth are completely dark. Light is so important to us that our eyes have evolved to where they are both sensitive to extremely low levels of light and able to operate in bright sunlight. In fact, we consider anyone who cannot see to be handicapped.

The source of light that we use most often to see with comes from our local star, the Sun. Hot objects glow, and the Sun is the hottest natural object in our solar system. It gives off mostly yellow light, but also blue, green, red, orange, and additional colors. This light travels through space, penetrates our atmosphere, and illuminates our world. But there is much more to light than what we see, and there are many more uses to which it can be put. First, it's necessary to try to understand exactly what light is and where it comes from.

PROPERTIES OF LIGHT: PHOTONS AND WAVES

We have all seen the glow from a fire, and we have all seen metal (such as the heating coils in a toaster or the burner in a stove or oven) turn red hot. If the metal's temperature keeps rising, the red glow turns orange, then yellow, and finally becomes white at the highest temperatures we can see. Light is made of particles called photons. Photons are given off by all objects at any temperature. In any object, the atoms (protons, neutrons, and electrons) that comprise it are in constant motion, vibrating and jiggling around. As they accelerate (speed up) and decelerate (slow down), the electrons constantly emit photons. Pumping heat into an object gives it more energy, which makes the atoms vibrate faster. The faster they vibrate, the shorter the wavelengths of light they give off. The shorter the wavelengths of light, the more energy it has.

An ordinary object at and just above room temperature gives off mostly infrared photons—this is how thermal imaging works. Heating something up to a few hundred degrees causes it to begin to glow red (red photons have more energy than infrared); heating that object can cause atoms and molecules to vibrate faster still and emit even shorter wavelengths. This makes sense if we consider how to make waves on a rope: Shaking a rope gently will only make a few waves along the rope; to create more waves (giving the waves a shorter wavelength) requires shaking the rope faster and, therefore, takes more work (energy).

Light is a wave of electromagnetic energy—a vibrating electromagnetic field moving through space. A light wave refracts and diffracts the same as a water wave or a sound wave, a process that has been seen in experiments going back for centuries. Rainbows are one example of this. Understanding the physics of a rainbow, as well as diffraction and refraction, make it clear that light is a wave.

Yet light is also a particle and a photon is a particle of light. There are also other experiments that clearly show that light acts as a particle. In fact, some experiments, if run one way, show that light is a particle, while other experiments, if run another way, show that light is a wave. Scientists have finally concluded that light is both a particle and a wave. Some experiments have revealed light's particle aspects, while other experiments have revealed its wavelike characteristics. In the same way, we can describe a car as being red, big, fast, or rusty—it depends on what characteristics we are interested in. When we see light reflecting, it helps to think of photons bouncing off of a mirror; and when photons are absorbed, it is also helpful to visualize, say, a tiny particle striking an electron and adding energy to it.

So, to review a little, here are some of fundamental properties of light. First, light has properties of both particles and waves: it can act like a particle (photon) that collides with other objects almost as if it is a tiny ball, or like a water wave that ripples through space and can split up and combine ("interfere") with other waves to create patterns. Second, light has important properties such as the wavelength—the distance between the crests of the wave. The wavelength, in turn, tells you the energy of the light—shorter-wavelength light (such as ultraviolet) has more energy, and longer-wavelength light (such as infrared) has lower energy. Third, light is part of a wide electromagnetic spectrum that includes not only the light we can see, but also a lot of radiation that is invisible to our eyes, such as X-rays and radio waves. Radio waves, X-rays, and visible light are all different forms of the same electromagnetic radiation.

Photons are absorbed by electrons, and electrons, in turn, emit photons. How this happens is actually very interesting. One thing to know, though, before we explore any further is that electrons are very picky—they can only exist at very specific distances from the center of an atom, as though they were planets orbiting the Sun. Each of these electron "orbitals" has a very precise energy. Therefore, for an electron to move from one orbital to a higher one requires a precise amount of energy—no more and no less than the energy it takes to move between these orbitals. Think of a staircase where each step is precisely 6 inches (15 centimeters) higher than the next lower step. If you want to move a ball from one step to the next, you have to lift it with enough energy to raise it at least 6 inches (15 cm)—if you raise the ball 5 inches (13 cm), it will fall back to where it started, and if you lift it with too much energy to where it rises 8 inches (20 cm), it will fall back 2 inches (5 cm) to end up one step higher. It works the same way with electrons—for an electron to jump to the next higher energy level, it needs a precise amount of energy, no more and no less.

In terms of photons, each photon has a precise amount of energy, no more and no less, and that energy is related to the wavelength of the photon. In fact, once we know the wavelength of a photon, we can calculate the precise energy it must have, and vice versa. Therefore, if we know the exact energy needed to raise an electron from one energy level to another, we can calculate the exact energy that a photon must have to make this change happen. We can also analyze light given off by an electron to tell precisely how far it fell from one energy level to a lower one. Raising an electron to a higher energy level is called **excitation,** and when the electron falls to a lower level (emitting light) it is called **de-excitation.** Thus, de-excitation makes an object glow at a very specific wavelength, while electrons that are being excited will absorb the very same specific wavelengths of light. And remember—wavelengths and energies are so closely related that to know one is to know the other. High energy means short wavelength, and low energy means long wavelength.

The other piece of the picture is that every type of atom is a little bit different—the energy levels for, say, a hydrogen atom are different than they are for an oxygen atom, and the energy levels for oxygen are different from those for iron. We can see some of this difference in the yellow light from streetlights, which comes from sodium vapor inside the lights, and the colors of the Northern Lights, which naturally occur with the release of photons from excited oxygen atoms and nitrogen molecules in the atmosphere (the green, for example, is given off by oxygen atoms). The colors in those beautiful photos of glowing gas clouds in space (called nebulae), come from de-exciting atoms of gas—green from oxygen, red from hydrogen, and so forth.

By measuring the spectrum of colors emitted by objects in space (and on Earth), scientists can tease out the exact chemical composition of whatever it is that they are studying. In fact, an odd collection of these colors (known as "spectral lines") that were discovered in the Sun led scientists to discover the existence of the Sun's helium (from the word *helios*, for "Sun") before that particular gas was ever found on Earth. In addition, astronomers also know that vast clouds of hydrogen gas are floating between the galaxies because they can see that certain colors are missing from the spectra of galaxies at the edge of the universe—the hydrogen in these clouds has absorbed some of the red light given off by the galaxies behind them. What we know about the composition of the universe we learn by studying the light that reaches us—or that is absorbed en route. Meanwhile, studying the light given off by atoms in earthbound laboratories helps us to better understand the properties of the atoms that are present in deep space.

When enough energy is added to an electron, it will not only jump up to a higher energy level, it will escape the atom altogether.

This principle explains how solar cells work: When sunlight hits electrons in a solar cell, it causes those electrons to escape from the atom; these escaped electrons are then sent through wires as electrical current. The process of adding enough energy to an electron to remove it altogether from an atom or molecule is called **ionization**.

The ionization process is used in many products. In a photocopier, for example, light shines on a piece of paper to be copied. The light that strikes text or images on the paper gets blocked, but the remaining light reaches a positively charged metal drum typically coated with atoms. The light ionizes the atoms and the removed electrons combine with the positive charges on the drum to make them electrically neutral. The remaining positively charged parts of the drum attract negatively charged toner (ink) particles, which form an imprint of the text or image, that is finally transferred to a piece of paper that rolls through. This method of using light to create ionization for making copies (among many other uses) takes advantage of the properties of light.

HOW LIGHT REVEALS THE WORLD: THE ELECTROMAGNETIC SPECTRUM

Atoms, with their complex array of electrons and energy levels, give off light at very discrete wavelengths—as we have seen, this pattern of wavelengths (emission and absorption lines) can be as distinctive as a fingerprint and can be used to identify those exact atomic elements that give off the light. But matter can also give off light across a smooth, continuous range of wavelengths—this is the glow that we see from the hot wires in a toaster, from the flames of a fire, and from the surface of the Sun.

Isaac Newton showed that sunlight contains every color of the rainbow. The breakdown of sunlight into its component colors shows us what is called the **spectrum** of the Sun. The range of colors that light contains goes far beyond what we can see in the solar spectrum. Light is an electromagnetic form of radiation, and the electromagnetic spectrum runs from radio waves (which have the longest wavelengths) to infrared, through visible light, and then on to ultraviolet, X-rays, and into gamma rays. This is called the electromagnetic

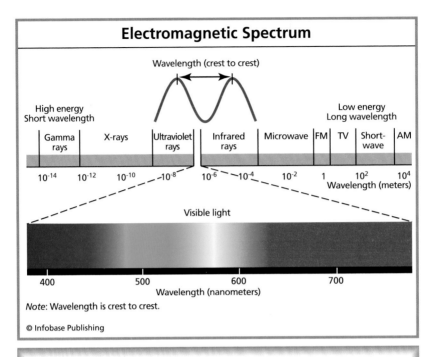

Figure 2.1 As shown in this image of the electromagnetic spectrum, higher energy corresponds to a shorter wavelength and higher frequency, while lower energy corresponds to longer wavelengths and lower frequency.

spectrum. The only difference between radio waves, visible light, and X-rays is the energy (and wavelength) of the radiation. Visible light has a shorter wavelength (and more energy) than radio waves, and X-rays have a shorter wavelength (and more energy) than visible light. There are many "colors" in the electromagnetic spectrum but our eyes can only see a small range of them, from red to violet. We cannot see radio waves or X-rays.

Now that we know that it takes more energy to create shorter wavelengths, we can learn something about the amount of energy—and, in turn, the temperature—of the atoms that are giving off the light. So, let's see how to put this knowledge to work!

Every object with a temperature gives off radiation, and if we study the spectrum of colors from that radiation on a graph, we will notice it has a characteristic shape. Most of the light emitted by the Sun, for example, is yellow—the Sun gives off lower-energy radiation (red, infrared, and radio wavelengths) as well as higher-energy radiation (blue, ultraviolet, and X-rays)—but anything with the temperature of the Sun will give off more yellow light than any other color. If we measure the amount of energy that the Sun gives off in each wavelength and plot it on a graph, we will see that the shape of this plot has a peak at yellow and drops off rapidly in both directions. In fact, if we heat up *any object* to the same temperature as the Sun, we'll see that the graph we plot has almost the same shape as the graph we plot for the Sun. This is called a radiation curve, and the exact shape of the radiation curve—the amount of light given off in each wavelength, and where the curve peaks—only depends on the temperature of the object. This means that measuring the shape of the curve, including identifying the peak, can tell us exactly how hot something is. Therefore, this helps add to our understanding of two concepts that were mentioned earlier: High-temperature objects give off more high-energy (short-wavelength) light, while low-temperature objects give off more low-energy (long-wavelength) light.

Say, for example, an astronomer is studying a cloud of gas in the depths of space. One way to study the gas is to see if it is absorbing or emitting specific wavelengths of light—from this, astronomers can tell what atomic elements make up the cloud of gas. Another way to study a gas cloud is to look at the radiation it emits. If the cloud is giving off visible light (like the Crab Nebula), then the temperature of the gas is in the thousands of degrees. If it is emitting mostly radio waves, then the gas is cold—maybe only a few degrees above absolute zero. Infrared light means that it is close to room temperature, while gas that is giving off X-rays is hot—millions of degrees. So, again, just measuring the radiation spectrum—the amount of energy given off in each wavelength—can tell us precisely how hot or cold something is, even when it is located halfway across the universe.

The light that is visible to the human eye is only a very tiny window in the entire electromagnetic spectrum. Unfortunately, the most interesting phenomena in the universe are hard to see in visible light. As a result, we need to use technology that will extend our senses into the ultraviolet, the infrared, radio, X-rays, and even gamma-ray wavelengths. In the past few decades, in fact, scientists have created many technological innovations to do this.

WORKING WITH LIGHT

Light is both a phenomenon and a tool. Light is used in industry and at home, in the laboratory and the operating room, and it plays a very important role in national defense—there are few areas in which light (often in the form of lasers) cannot be used. Working with light is not new: The first **lenses** date back at least 3,000 years. (The earliest known examples seem to have been used as magnifying glasses and for creating fires.) They have been used throughout history by Assyrians, ancient Egyptians, ancient Greeks, Romans, Arabs, and Vikings (among others) through the centuries. And, until recently, humanity's use of light was limited to manipulating it with lenses to help us see better (microscopes, eyeglasses, telescopes), or focusing sunlight on flammable materials to start fires.

Today, lenses are incredibly important. More than ever, we make eyeglasses to see with, microscopes to magnify infinitesimally small objects, and telescopes to bring into close view objects located far away. Today, lenses are also used to focus lasers into pinpoints that can be used to scan CDs and DVDs, as well as bar codes at the supermarket. They can also be used in submarine periscopes for surveying, photography, and much more.

Manipulating light with lenses was the primary way that humanity used light for millennia. This did not really change until the middle part of the nineteenth century with the discovery of the **photoelectric effect** in which light ejects electrons from a material, such as a metal surface. At this time, light began to be much more useful.

Although the photoelectric effect was not really explained until 1905 (Albert Einstein was the first to understand it; his explanation won him his Nobel Prize), it was first noticed in 1839 by French scientist Alexandre Becquerel. About a half century later, scientists Heinrich Hertz, JJ Thomson, and Nikolai Tesla all found ways to make use of this effect. In 1902, Philipp von Lenard was the first to realize that blue light produced more electrical current than yellow light, and that ultraviolet (UV) light produced even more current than blue.

The discovery of the photoelectric effect made all sorts of inventions possible. Solar cells, for example, depend on it. In addition to producing electrical power for homes, solar cells power watches, calculators, small lights, and so forth. The photoelectric effect is widely used elsewhere, although many people don't realize it. Anytime a bell rings when someone enters a store, there's a chance that a photocell is involved—a beam of light shining across the doorway onto a photocell is broken by the customer walking through the door. This creates the signal to sound a chime. The photoelectric effect is also used as a safety device (to keep garage doors from crushing people, for example), to check to make sure that soda bottles in factories are full enough, and more. The photoelectric effect is also used in electronic devices called photodiodes and phototransistors, and variations of the photoelectric effect are used in television cameras, home video cameras, and digital cameras. These devices (called CCDs, for "charge-coupled devices") will be discussed in the next section, along with lasers and scanners.

In addition to these inventions, the photoelectric effect can actually be important in space exploration. The photoelectric effect happens when sunlight hits moon dust; it causes the dust to develop an electric charge. This dust actually rises off the Moon's surface to create a very slight haze that was seen by some of the earliest astronauts. (The smallest dust particles might rise as high as a few kilometers.) Satellites and spacecraft experience something related to this: The photoelectric effect can cause the sunlit side of a spacecraft (or satellite) to develop an electrical charge of a few tens of volts. At the same time, the shaded side of the craft can actually develop a high negative charge from other phenomena. Whenever there is both a positive and negative charge, electrical current will try to flow to help balance the charges out. This current flow can pass through delicate electronic components inside the spacecraft and cause problems.

Everything previously discussed deals with visible light, but there is a lot more to light than just what can be seen by the human eye. Remember that visible light is only a small part of the entire electromagnetic spectrum. In addition to devices that use (or make use of) visible light, any technology that uses radio waves is also using part of the electromagnetic spectrum. Therefore, radar guns, cell phones, radio and television stations, wireless computer connections (in fact, anything that communicates wirelessly) all use long wavelengths at the lower end of the electromagnetic spectrum. At the top end, UV light is used to etch the patterns on silicon chips to make computer chips; it also helps to make plastics dry and set up more quickly. X-rays are used to help diagnose broken bones, to find cavities, and for other medical purposes (as well as to find defects that might cause pipes to burst or buildings to collapse). And gamma rays are used to help treat some diseases as well as in research and for making images (called radiography). As we can see, modern technology has found a use for every part of the electromagnetic spectrum. And, as we will see later, the same can be said for astronomers who currently use both ground and space telescopes to observe the spectrums in the universe from radio waves through gamma rays. No wavelength goes uninvestigated and unobserved.

LASERS, CCDS, AND SCANNERS

One of the most important uses for light is in **lasers** (laser stands for Light Amplification by the Stimulated Emission of Radiation). Lasers were actually predicted by Einstein in 1917, but were not actually invented until 1960 (by Theodore Maiman). Even then, nobody really knew what to do with them until the mid-1970s. (Nobel Laureate Charles Townes, who invented a microwave version of the laser, called a maser, said that, for many years, some people told him that the laser was "a solution looking for a problem.")

Eventually, however, uses were found for the laser—more and more uses, in fact, as time went on, and lasers became easier and less expensive to manufacture. Today, virtually everyone encounters lasers on a daily basis when they turn on CD and DVD players, get in line at the supermarket checkout, use a laser pointer during a presentation, and anytime they place a call (or download a file) over a fiber-optic data line.

Think about how lasers work. As we noted earlier, photons are given off by electrons when they fall from a higher energy level to a lower one. With a laser, a lot of electrons become excited; this excitation lifts them into a higher energy level (this is sometimes called "pumping"). Then, when a photon of the right energy passes an atom with an excited electron, the electric field of the passing photon can induce the excited electrons to hop back down to a lower energy level, emitting a photon of exactly the same wavelength as the passing photon—this is what is called stimulated emission. The process can be continued, for example, by making a mirror in which the photons can bounce back and forth between the atoms, and the

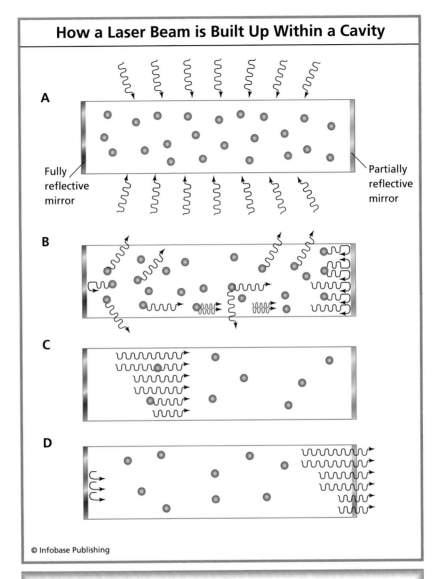

How a Laser Beam is Built Up Within a Cavity

A

Fully
reflective
mirror

Partially
reflective
mirror

B

C

D

© Infobase Publishing

Figure 2.2   In (a), the laser medium absorbs energy, and then in (b), it begins emitting photons. After stimulated emission, the photons form a coherent wave, as seen in (c). In (d), they exit upon reaching high intensity.

beam keeps growing in strength. Some of the photons are allowed to escape through the mirror and form a beam. To keep the beam going, the electrons are re-excited so that the stimulated emission continues for as long as power is applied to continue exciting the electrons.

One of the many jobs that lasers are used for is scanning, and the most familiar form of this is the barcode scanner seen by shoppers at the supermarket checkout (among many other places). Barcode scanners are actually the easiest way to scan with light: All a scanner needs is a light source, a device such as a photocell to measure the reflected light, and a way to know the position of the light and dark spots. So, in the case of a barcode scanner, when a laser (the light source) is scanned across a series of light and dark bars, the light is reflected by the white spaces and is absorbed by the dark lines; a photocell (or other light-measuring device) records whether a lot or a little light is reflected back from the barcode while the computer keeps track of where the laser was pointing when it sensed the light and dark areas. In the case of barcode scanners, the process is easy—recognizing light and dark areas is all that's necessary.

A computer scanner, in addition to recognizing light and dark, is also able to recognize colors and to scan each line and assemble all of the lines together into a single picture (this is what happens with television and computer monitors as well). The biggest complication with a computer's scanner is the process of recognizing colors, and recognizing small enough pixels to form a high-quality picture.

Taking scanning to even greater sophistication, there are laser scanners that create a three-dimensional reproduction of an object. The light from these scanners is reflected through a lens to a sensor that is able to determine the exact three-dimensional shape of the object being scanned. Holograms, which also use lasers to generate three-dimensional images, are made using a different principle—the interference between laser beams. And, in some cases, these three-dimensional images can be used to re-create a solid object—lasers can be used to *sinter* (fuse together) fine particles of plastic in a precise pattern to form a solid object that exactly matches what was scanned. Sintering has been used to create, for example, reproductions of very valuable and very fragile antiques so that the reproductions can be put on display in museums while the irreplaceable originals are kept safe and secure.

Barcode and Pattern Table

3 1117 01320 6375

Pattern Table			
Character	Pattern	Bars	Spaces
0	1111	0001	001
1	1111	0010	001
2	1111	0001	010
3	1111	1000	100
4	1111	0100	001
5	1111	1000	001
6	1111	0001	100
7	1111	0010	100
8	1111	0100	100
9	1111	1000	010
–	1111	0010	010
$	1111	0100	010
:	1111	1011	000
/	1111	1101	000
.	1111	1110	000
+	1111	0111	000
A or T	1111	0100	011
B or N	1111	0001	110
C or *	1111	0001	011
D or E	1111	0010	011

Figure 2.3 A laser barcode scanner uses light to scan a barcode's series of lines. Then, using the information in the table, which is already programmed into the scanner, the scanner will read the encoded product number.

Figure 2.4 Physics Nobel Prize laureates Willard S. Boyle (*left*) and George E. Smith, both Americans working at Bell Laboratories in Murray Hill, New Jersey, take part in a press conference at the Royal Academy of Sciences in Stockholm, Sweden, on December 7, 2009.

Light can also be used with a tool called a charge-coupled device (CCD). Similar to computer chips, CCDs are used in digital cameras, video cameras, astronomical observatories, and virtually anything else that electronically records an image. Although the idea of digital photography was first suggested in 1961 by Eugene Lally (who proposed using it for spacecraft guidance), the CCD was first developed in 1969 by Bell Labs scientists Willard Boyle and George Smith, who suggested using them for picture phones. Boyle and Smith shared the 2009 Nobel Prize in physics for their pioneering work.

The CCD works by focusing an image on a CCD chip, just as an image can be focused on film in a camera. But, instead of film, the CCD has an array of capacitors, which are electronic devices that collect and hold an electrical charge. The photons hit the capacitors and cause electrons to be ejected via the photoelectric effect. Every time a photon hits one of these capacitors (called a well) a very small

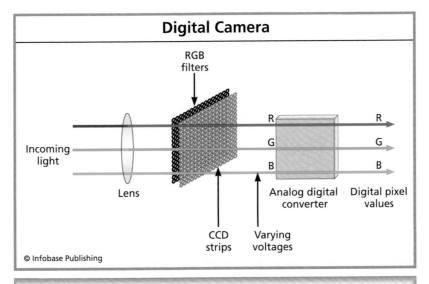

Digital Camera

RGB filters

Incoming light

Lens

CCD strips

Varying voltages

Analog digital converter

Digital pixel values

R G B   R G B

© Infobase Publishing

Figure 2.5   Digital cameras use a charge-coupled device (CCD) to convert incoming light to varying voltages that are digitized to create pixel values.

electrical charge is deposited. Adding up the charge in a well tells the camera how many photons struck—how bright the light was in that particular spot. Then, all of these spots are put together to form a picture. To extract the picture from the CCD is not necessarily simple, but it is fairly straightforward (Figure 2.5). The charge in one corner of the CCD is read out, then the charge in the rest of the wells on this row are passed to the right, and each is read out in turn—like passing a bucket from person to person along a line. When the bottommost row has been read out, the charges in all the higher rows are passed down a row and the whole process begins again. After all of the wells have been read out, the photo is complete and stored in the camera (or computer) memory. Digital camera photos take a few seconds to "develop" because it takes time to read out all of the pixels and record the information. All devices that use a CCD (video cameras, digital cameras, astronomical cameras, scanners, etc.) record information and work in the same way. A scanner is essentially the same as a one-line CCD, scanning a single line at a time and assembling the image by moving the scanner bar across the image to be recorded.

(continues on page 36)

Light Travels Through Nothing: Michelson-Morley Experiment

Water waves travel through water. Sound waves travel through air. Seismic waves move through rock. Every sort of wave that scientists could understand appeared to move through something—every sort of wave seemed to need a substance to travel through.

When it came to studying light, it was only natural to assume that, if it was a wave, then it, too, must travel through something. This was easy enough to see when experiments were run on Earth—the light would be traveling through water or air or glass. But physicists and astronomers knew, too, that light traveled across vast distances in space—from the planets and stars to our eyes—and they knew that space was apparently empty. So how, they wondered, could light waves travel if there was nothing for them to travel through?

For a few centuries, this question wasn't really seen as a problem. Isaac Newton assumed that light was "corpuscular," meaning that it was made of little particles (which he called "corpuscles"). Like meteors, planets, and rocks, little corpuscles of light could easily travel through space. But over time, it became obvious that light acted like a wave, and all waves (or so the thinking went) needed something to travel through. This realization raised serious questions. Physicists finally concluded that even "empty" space must be filled with a substance, which they called "aether," that was thin enough for planets to move through but could also vibrate enough to permit the transmission of light waves. So, for decades, scientists turned their attention to trying to detect this aether.

The matter was finally settled by a brilliant experiment in 1887—one of the most important experiments in the history of science—designed by American physicists Albert Michelson and Edward Morley. Michelson and Morley figured that if the Earth moved through the aether, light traveling in the direction of the Earth's motion would behave

Figure 2.6 Physicist Albert A. Michelson invented the interferometer to discover the effect of Earth's motion on the observed velocity. The instrument also enabled distances to be measured by means of the length of light waves, which provided greater accuracy than ever before.

differently than light traveling at right angles to that motion. By finding a way to detect this difference, they could prove that the aether existed, and they found a brilliant method of carrying out this experiment—by using reflecting light from mirrors.

They started with the fact that the Earth is in orbit around the Sun, and the Sun is in orbit around the galaxy. (Michelson and Morley didn't realize that the galaxy is also in motion through the universe, but that was not essential to their experiment.) What is even more important is that the Earth is in motion through the universe; if the universe is filled with aether, there should be a constant "wind" blowing by the Earth at all times, and the direction and speed of this wind should change as the Earth orbits the Sun. Furthermore, if this wind was what allowed light

(continues)

(continued)

to travel through space, the speed of light should be affected by the speed of the aether wind through which it shone—just as the speed of a bullet is affected (even if only very slightly) by the speed of the wind. So Michelson and Morley shot off a beam of light and then used the mirrors to split it into two beams that traveled at right angles to each other. On the one hand, if the Earth was really moving through an aether wind, the beams should take very slightly different amounts of time to travel these paths; and if the light waves were all exactly the same frequency and all of the waves were in step with each other, then recombining the beams should show no difference when compared to a single beam. On the other hand, even the slightest amount of an aether wind would cause the beams to be just the smallest bit out of phase with each other (in other words, the crests and troughs from one beam would not line up exactly with the crests and troughs from the other beam, and they would cancel out to some degree).

Michelson and Morley fully expected to see out-of-phase light, which would prove the existence of the aether and help them to calculate its speed past the Earth. To their amazement they found—nothing! The beams' path lengths were the same, so they lined up exactly when they recombined. After incredibly careful testing, they could only conclude that there was no aether—and their experiment (which earned Michelson the 1907 Nobel Prize in physics) is called the most famous experiment that failed. Light could, it turned out, travel through absolutely nothing.

(continued from page 33)

OTHER WAYS OF MAKING LIGHT: LIGHT BULBS, CATHODE RAY TUBES, AND LEDS

Many of these devices won't work without some way of making light. The way that lasers produce light has already been described, but there are other ways of making photons.

The oldest way of making light is called **incandescence**. This process produces light from a heated object, such as the heating of a wire filament until it glows. The heated wire glows, giving off enough light to heat up a room, a street, or a stadium. Old-fashioned light bulbs work this way.

Another tried-and-true process for making light is **fluorescence**, which is seen in the tube-type light bulbs seen in schools and stores. In a fluorescent light, mercury atoms are in a vapor; the atoms are excited by an electrical field so that they give off UV light. The UV is not only invisible, but is dangerous as well. For this reason, the tubes are covered with a phosphor—a material that absorbs the UV light and emits longer-wavelength visible light that we can see. Fluorescent light bulbs are a lot more efficient and use a lot less energy than old-fashioned ones.

Phosphorescence and fluorescence are responsible for a lot of the light found on Earth, including much of the world's natural light. Many minerals are fluorescent—they glow brightly under UV light, which is used to help identify them. Molecules can be fluorescent, which is what helps fireflies and some jellyfish to glow. In fact, these molecules can be put into organisms and cells to help understand how they work. This development was so important that three scientists who studied this jellyfish molecule, known as green fluorescent protein, won the 2008 Nobel Prize in chemistry.

Phosphorescence is also at work in many televisions and computer monitors—not the flat-panel displays, which use liquid crystals or plasma to generate a picture, but the older cathode ray-type displays. In a cathode ray tube, high-energy electrons strike phosphors in the screen, causing them to glow. The electron beam is rapidly turned on and off as it is scanned from side to side, lighting up individual pixels as it scans. (This is similar to the way that a CCD is read out.) And, as happens with a CCD, a picture is built up from all of the individual spots of light, which are known as "pixels" (short for "picture elements").

Another way to make light is by the use of electronic components called **light-emitting diodes** (LEDs). Unlike other types of light bulbs, which rely on some sort of gas or non-solid material, an LED is a small bit of solid material (an electrical semiconductor). It is "doped" with "impurities," which are additional atoms that don't normally exist in the material. These impurities cause the semiconductor to give off light when an electrical current passes through. And, because it is individual electrons around specific atoms that are being excited, you might guess that each LED will give off a very specific color—the first LEDs were red, but there are now blue, UV, green, and even white LEDs. Other solid-state light emitters have been developed as well, such as diodes that emit laser light. Laser diodes are, in fact, found in virtually every home in the United States—they are what emit the lasers that are used in CD and DVD players, as well as every computer that contains of these devices.

Laser diodes are among the most common light-emitting devices made on Earth; only light bulbs and fluorescent lights are more common. LEDs are important because they provide the most efficient way yet found to produce light and they are growing less and less expensive—LED flashlights that can be powered by hand-cranking a very small electrical generator are beginning to show up in the developing world, enabling billions of people to see in the dark without burning a fire or running an electrical generator.

There are other ways of making light, just as there are other ways of using it, but going into all of these would take up several books or a full database of information. For now, we will leave this subject and find out a little more about sound.

What Sound Is and How It Can Be Used

We live a life that is as immersed in sound as in light. Even in absolute darkness and absolute silence we can hear and feel our heartbeat and the sound of our breath. Sound is a part of the life of everyone on Earth from before they are born (fetuses in the womb can hear and feel sounds) until the moment of death. Given that, it is no surprise that we depend heavily on sound to communicate and to alert us to both opportunity and danger (the sound of a cracking branch, for example, could signal the presence of either tonight's dinner, or a bear).

On the face of it, sound is rather simple—it is nothing more (or less) than waves of pressure moving through air, water, or some other substance. What makes these waves into sound is that they are able to interact with our ears in such a way that they produce nerve signals.

There are sounds that no one can hear, just as there are wavelengths of light we cannot see. And, just as we have with those wavelengths of light, we have found ways to detect and to use these inaudible parts of the sonic spectrum. And, as with light, we have also found ways to use the audible wavelengths.

PROPERTIES OF SOUND

Pluck a rubber band and look at it. Chances are that you'll see the rubber band moving rapidly back and forth, and you may hear a low humming sound. If you listen closely, you may even hear the humming get lower and softer as the rubber band's vibrations slow down until finally they become too low or too soft to hear.

Think of moving your hand rapidly through the water. Water piles up in front of your hand, while a small trough forms behind it. Move your hand rapidly back and forth and you'll see this happen alternately in front of and behind your hand—water piles up in the direction of motion, and there's always a little less water behind. This is exactly what happens with the rubber band, except that it is moving the air instead of water—air piles up in front of the rubber band as it moves forward while the air in the back is slightly less dense. This is an example of how sound works: alternating waves of pressure going through the air (or water or solid objects). If the waves are very close to each other (because the rubber band is vibrating quickly) we hear a high-pitched sound. More widely spaced sound waves produce low rumbles. The speed at which the rubber band vibrates—its frequency—is what controls the sound that we hear.

The human ear can hear frequencies ranging from 20 Hz (20 cycles per second) all the way up to 20,000 Hz. Yet, as our ears get older, they start to lose the highest frequencies but remain sensitive to the lower ones. This is a tremendous range of frequencies, far greater than the range of wavelengths that our eyes can see. Remember that the wavelength depends not only on the frequency of a wave, but also on the speed at which it travels. Since the speed of sound varies quite a bit as it travels through different substances, it makes more sense to talk about sound in terms of frequency because the same wavelength will sound different under different circumstances. This is why, for example, people's voices sound funny after they inhale helium—the speed of sound is faster in helium than it is in air, but our **vocal folds** stay the same length and vibrate at the same speed. Thus, the same wavelength of a sound wave (which is controlled by the length and vibration of our vocal folds) makes a squeaky sound when we breathe helium through our throats than when we breathe air. Having said that, the sounds that humans can hear at sea level have wavelengths that measure anywhere from about one-half inch (1 cm) to more than 55 feet (17 m) between crests.

Sound, then, is a series of pressure waves that vibrate at the right frequency so that they register in our ears (more on how that happens shortly). So, like any other wave, sound can be characterized by having a frequency (remember, this is the number of wave crests that pass by every second), a wavelength, and a speed. In addition, sound can have power behind it—it can be loud or soft. With the softest sounds, our eardrums may move only a fraction of a millionth of a millimeter, yet we hear the sound. The loudest sounds make our entire body feel like it's being pummeled. In fact, some whales use sound to stun their prey; there is also concern that military sonar systems are, in turn, doing harm to whales. When U.S. submarines are stationed in a port where security is questionable, they will periodically use their active sonar to dissuade potential saboteurs, a manuever that may cause whales, dolphins, and other sea creatures' deaths.

Like light, sound has a speed at which it travels, but this speed can vary quite a bit depending on what the sound is traveling through—the denser the medium, the faster the speed of sound. In air at sea level, sound travels at about 767 miles (1,234 km) per hour; in the cold, dry, thinner air at the altitude of commercial airliners, it slows down to 660 miles (1,062 km) per hour. In seawater, by comparison, sound can move at more than 3,300 miles (5,310 km) per hour, and it moves even faster through steel. Sound waves from an earthquake will travel through the entire Earth in less than an hour, moving at up to 11,000 miles (17,702 km) per hour.

Now it's time to put all of this information together to think about some common phenomena. But, to keep this discussion relatively simple, we'll assume that the speed of the sound is the same. Music seems like a good place to start—with string instruments leading the way.

PLAYING FOR SOUND

A violin string (or a guitar string, or any other string) is a lot more like a rubber band than you might think at first, with the biggest difference being that rubber bands are easier to stretch. When a guitar string is plucked (or if a violin string is rubbed with the bow) it vibrates the same way the rubber band does. And, like the rubber band, the sound that it makes depends on how quickly the string vibrates—this vibration is a standing wave (just like the guitar string mentioned in the first section). Thus, the difference between a high note and a lower one lies in the vibration speed of the guitar string.

All things being equal, a longer string will vibrate more slowly (giving a lower musical note) than a shorter one. Looking at a guitar (or any other string instrument), we can see that some strings are longer than others. This is part of the reason that a guitar or violin can be made to produce different notes, simply by having different lengths of the strings.

In addition, we see that some strings are thicker than others; this is also important. A thicker string is heavier and doesn't move as quickly as a thin string—so thicker strings give off lower notes than thin ones. This means that the lowest notes should come from the thickest and longest strings, which is exactly how string instruments are built (or "strung"). The musician can make the strings even shorter by holding them down with their fingers to play still higher notes. Turning the pegs (the knobs at the end of the neck) to make a string tight also raises the pitch. A lot of thought goes into designing the strings of a violin or guitar: the length, thickness, and even the material that the strings are made of, and how tightly they are stretched. All these factors affect the sound that a string instrument makes.

All string instruments make sound the same way—by setting up vibrations in a string and then controlling their frequency with a combination of string length, weight, and the tension put on them. The strings on a guitar and banjo are plucked; violin, cello, viola, and bass strings are played with a bow (though they can also be plucked); harps are strummed with the fingers; and piano strings are struck with felted hammers. But, once the vibrations are started, the same methods are used to control the sound that the strings make.

Wind instruments (and organ pipes), however, work differently. All wind instruments (and a pipe organ is a type of wind instrument) operate pretty much the same way. (For that matter, anyone who creates a sound by blowing across the top of a soda bottle is making a primitive wind instrument.) In all of them, the air molecules are made to vibrate, and a standing wave—what we hear as a musical note—is set up in some sort of pipe. With a reed instrument, such as a clarinet, bassoon, oboe, or saxophone, blowing across a reed causes it to vibrate and those vibrations establish a standing wave in the pipe, which forms the rest of the instrument. Opening and closing holes along the length of the instrument changes the length

Figure 3.1 Guitar strings vibrate when plucked. The different lengths of strings, which can be tightened or loosened on the frame to change the tones they produce affect vibration speed and, thus, the sound that is produced.

of the air column that the sound waves occupy and, as with a vibrating string, changes the note that is played. With a flute, the standing wave is caused by blowing across a hole at the end of the instrument, which causes the air to vibrate. (Flutes carved from bone are believed to be the first musical instruments, made as far back in history as 43,000 years ago.)

In the case of brass instruments, the vibrations come when players buzz their lips on the mouthpiece. The length of the tube is changed by opening and shutting valves (except in a slide trombone, where the length of the pipe is changed by using the slide).

In each of these, the principle is the same—a longer pipe allows the production of a longer standing wave to produce a lower (deeper) tone. This is the most obvious in an organ, where every individual musical note is produced by a different pipe, and each pipe is physically longer or shorter, wider or narrower. In an organ, we can see the difference in the notes by simply looking at the size of the pipes.

This same principle applies to human voices, by the way. The voice is produced by small buzzing flaps of tissue—our vocal folds—located inside of the **larynx**, or voice box. Adults have longer vocal folds and deeper voices than children; men have larger voice boxes and deeper voices than women. With stereo speakers, deeper notes emerge from larger speakers, which is why the subwoofer is bigger than the tweeter. Again, the basic principles of making sound in all of these are the same.

WORKING WITH SOUND

Sound can't be picked up and held, it can't be molded into shape, and it can't be machined on a lathe. Like light, sound is fleeting, passing through an object on its way from here to there. This makes sound difficult to work with—but not impossible. Like light, sound can be produced, manipulated, amplified, focused, and absorbed.

We have already discussed a few ways of producing sound. Every method of making sound relies on the same principles of creating a vibration in some object and letting that vibration produce the sound frequency (or frequencies) that are needed. But the range of sounds that can be produced, and the way that these sounds can be used, is truly phenomenal. Take sonar, for example.

Sonar is used by submarines; just about everyone has seen movies where a submarine is "pinging"—sending a pulse of sound into the water—to try to detect an enemy submarine. Active sonar is used for finding the exact location of an object. To accomplish this, the submarine sends a pulse of sound into the water. Any object in the sound pulse's path will reflect part of that sound back to the submarine. By measuring the speed of sound in water (something that submarines do constantly) and timing the lag between sending and receiving a return pulse, a submarine can determine its distance from the other sub. For example, if the sound is moving at 2 miles (3.2 km) per second through the water and it takes six seconds for the pulse to return, this means that the sound has traveled 12 miles (19 km), so the other sub must be half that distance—6 miles (nearly 10 km)—away.

However, knowing the distance solves only part of the problem: The submarine must also know the bearing (in which direction the

Figure 3.2 A pipe organ produces sound when buttons on a keyboard are pushed to move pressurized air through pipes of different lengths.

other sub is located) if it is to maneuver to avoid or attack the enemy. To accomplish this, every submarine uses a bank of **hydrophones**—highly sensitive underwater microphones—that can detect sound very precisely in virtually every direction in front and to the sides (most submarines have problems listening to what is directly behind them because the submarine blocks the sound). Those hydrophones that are pointed directly toward the other submarine will hear the loudest sounds, while the sound in other hydrophones will not be quite as loud. By putting all of this information together, the sonar computer can determine the bearing of the target.

Active sonar is a great tool, but it has an important drawback—an enemy can hear it, too. A submarine's active sonar can locate enemy subs up to 10 or 20 miles (16 to 32 km) away, but that same sonar can be detected from more than 30 miles (48 km) distant—like a flashlight, which can be seen much further away than its useful light can reach. Active sonar is also complex—it takes a lot of computer power to figure out the exact distance and bearing to the target. Not only that, nature invented sonar first. Every bat and every whale are living sonar units, and their sonar puts ours to shame. Whales (including dolphins and orcas) generate sound in organs in their heads and broadcast it through the water; the returning sound tells them the exact location of the fish (or what object the sound reflected from). Dolphins and other toothed whales can tell the difference between various species of fish, and some species can even stun their prey with focused sound.

As good as dolphins are at acoustic navigation, bats are even better. In spite of the fact that air is far worse than water at conducting sound, bat sonar is far more precise and gives much better resolution (meaning it can detect smaller objects) than can whale sonar. Bat sonar can pick out individual insects and even help bats fly between closely spaced wires without touching them. When it comes to using sound for navigation and for hunting, human beings take a back seat to nature's best. But there is much more to using sound than broadcasting and listening to sonar.

Believe it or not, sound is very good at cleaning things. If you don't keep up with your brushing and flossing, the dentist might use a sonic probe to clean your teeth. Jewelers sometimes project strong sound waves into water tanks to clean the grime from jewelry—a

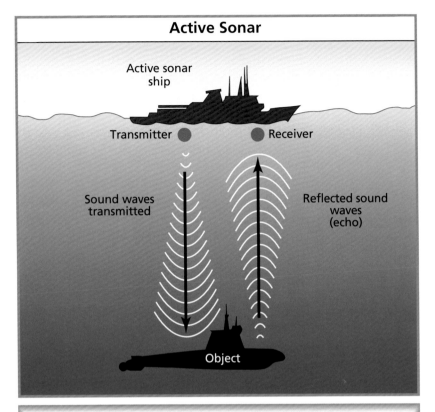

Active Sonar

Active sonar ship

Transmitter ● ● Receiver

Sound waves transmitted

Reflected sound waves (echo)

Object

Figure 3.3   Ships use active sonar techniques—emitting pulses of sounds and listening for echoes—to locate objects underwater, navigate, and communicate with other vessels.

technique that is sometimes used in factories as well. Sound waves are caused by vibrating material, but they can also cause vibrations when they are absorbed. If these vibrations are strong enough, they can vibrate off the dirt and grime, leaving a ring (or whatever) sparkling clean. Most of the time, the frequencies are **ultrasonic**—a higher frequency than any person can hear. The next section will further discuss ultrasound (and its opposite number, **infrasound**—sound too low-pitched for anyone to hear).

The principles of sonar can be used to study objects, as well. Sound waves can be used to probe pipes and steel walls for flaws. High-frequency sound waves reflect differently from small bubbles and cracks than they do from solid metal. By carefully monitoring the sound waves sent into a steel pipe (and those that are reflected back) a tester can tell if a pipe is solid or if it is about to break. After an earthquake, this same sort of testing can help find out if a building's steel I-beams are still strong enough to hold the building up. (This sort of "nondestructive testing" can be used on anything solid.) Geologists use sound to create images of rock layers to both look for a range of minerals and other substances from gold to oil and to advance their understanding of the layers of rock beneath our feet.

What all of these methods have in common is that they all send sound waves into objects and then interpret the reflections. Think of looking through a window—most of the light passes through the glass, but some of it reflects back. Sound works the same way—some sound energy will reflect back from flaws within a metal. Sound will also reflect back from any boundaries—say, where two metal plates are bolted together, or where metal is fastened to wood. Each of these boundaries will return an echo, as will a far wall. By using sonic impulses, a skilled technician can tell exactly how thick an object is (to see if it is starting to weaken or corrode), look for defects, and identify all of the different layers within.

One of the most interesting new sonic phenomena is something called **sonoluminescence**—the conversion of sound waves into light. In the period between World War I and World War II, scientists working on sonar systems thought that beaming high levels of ultrasound into liquids would speed up chemical reactions in them (and, in fact, this does happen), but they also noticed it also caused bubbles in the liquid to release light. It wasn't until the 1980s, however, that the process came under scientific scrutiny. In the 1990s, research began in earnest.

Most water contains tiny bubbles of air. These bubbles can capture and focus the energy from the sound wave—when that happens, the gas inside the bubbles heats up and the bubbles expand. This lasts for only a moment—a few tens of microseconds to be exact (a microsecond is one millionth of a second). After that, the bubbles start to collapse at a rate very close to the speed of sound until the gas inside is so dense that the collapse slams to a stop. As the bubbles shrink, the gas inside heats up to tens of thousands of degrees—maybe even hotter—and glows from the heat. Even though these bubbles glow blue, they emit even more light in the UV. Collapsing a small bubble at such high speeds doesn't take very long—the flash of light is over in just a few picoseconds (a picosecond is a millionth of a millionth of a second). Then the bubble returns to its original size and waits for the next sound impulse.

Some researchers think that the temperatures might rise even higher—possibly even high enough to cause hydrogen atoms within the bubble to fuse. The evidence for this is not firm, though. Out of the many scientific teams who have been studying this effect, only one or two to date have seen what they think might be evidence of fusion. The way things work in science is that, if an experiment can't be repeated successfully by other scientists, the results are not seen as conclusive. Until more groups of scientists also uncover evidence of hydrogen fusion, it's doubtful that anyone else will accept its existence. At this time, scientists are still trying to understand the potential of sonoluminescence and how it might be used. There are not many uses for it yet, but it's a neat phenomenon!

ULTRASOUND AND INFRASOUND

As with light, we can only hear a small part of the sonic spectrum; frequencies that are too low to hear are called infrasound (sometimes they're called "subsonic" frequencies), while ultrasound refers to those frequencies that are too high-pitched to register in our ears. Even though we can't hear infrasound, we can feel it. Experiments have shown that people can sense infrasound. Playing tones just below people's normal hearing range has been shown to cause feelings of anxiety, fear, and other odd sensations. Some researchers think that some buildings that are thought of as haunted might actually contain infrasound sources that create those unusual "haunted" feelings that some people experience. One engineer, named Vic Tandy, even noticed that he was experiencing feelings of dread whenever he was in his laboratory and thought he was seeing things that weren't there. He later discovered that the dimensions of his laboratory were almost exactly the same as the wavelength of an infrasonic wave and was able to prove that a blowing fan was creating a standing wave of infrasound in his laboratory. In addition, the frequency of this wave (18.98 Hz) was almost exactly the same frequency that causes an eyeball to vibrate. This led him to suspect that this same standing wave was causing his eyes to vibrate, causing him to see ghostly images.

Some animals—elephants, hippos, and giraffes, for example—seem to communicate with infrasound. This infrasound can travel much greater distances than the frequencies that we can hear. Infrasonic waves are given off by thunderstorms, tornadoes, earthquakes, and even tsunamis, among other natural events. Many people have noticed that animals seem able to "predict" natural disasters. This could be because they are hearing and reacting to the infrasound associated with these events. A method of detecting distant nuclear explosions uses the infrasound that is given off by any large detonation. All in all, for something that can't even be sensed, infrasound turns out to be pretty useful—not only to humans, but to the animal kingdom as well.

As useful as infrasound is, ultrasound turns out to be even more valuable to us. Some of the uses of sound that were mentioned in the previous section are performed by ultrasound: Ultrasonic cleaning tools are used to remove dirt and grime and ultrasonic probes are used to detect flaws in metal. A very quickly vibrating metal plate can force water molecules into the air—this is the principle of ultrasonic humidifiers, which don't need to heat the water. There is also a small field of scientific study called *sonochemistry*, in which ultrasound is used to help create chemical reactions in liquids that don't occur readily on their own. And there is growing interest in using ultrasound to help kill bacteria by breaking them apart. This technique has been used to help sterilize sewage. The same process may one day help to process corn to help make forming ethanol more efficient.

Still, the best-known use of ultrasound is probably in medicine. Ultrasound has been used to look inside the human body for at least a half century, mostly to examine developing babies to make sure that they are healthy. Ultrasound is also used examine the heart and major blood vessels to see if the blood is flowing properly. Sound travels differently through healthy and unhealthy tissues, so ultrasound can also help detect and identify damage inside the body. And, even more recently, ultrasound has been found to help drugs reach the brain so they work more effectively. It also seems to help broken bones heal more quickly.

Medical Ultrasound

Substance	Speed of ultrasound (m/s)
Air	334
Bone	3,360
Fat	1,476
Muscle	1,540
Saline gel	1,515

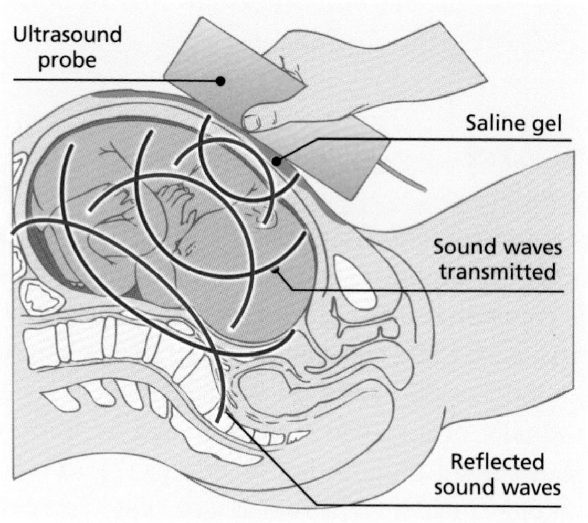

Ultrasound probe

Saline gel

Sound waves transmitted

Reflected sound waves

Figure 3.4   Ultrasound is produced as cyclic sound pressure with a frequency greater than the upper limit of human hearing. There are many different medical uses for ultrasound.

Of course, just because people can't hear ultrasound doesn't mean that it is inaudible to all animals. In fact, many animals use it all the time. Dogs, for example, can hear the ultrasonic frequencies from dog whistles even though we can't. Bats use ultrasound for their navigation systems. While the most we ever hear from bats is a high-pitched squeaking, the ultrasonic frequencies help them paint a rich picture of their surroundings. (Moths, which bats eat, also seem to be able to hear ultrasound, which helps them dodge the bats that are hunting for them.) Dolphins and other whales (and some of the fish they hunt) can hear ultrasonic frequencies, as well. Even mice, as has been recently discovered, sing to each other using ultrasonic frequencies.

As we've seen, just because we can't hear sound doesn't make it useless—there may be more uses for infrasound and ultrasound than there are for the audible frequencies. Not only that, but animals use these frequencies to communicate over long distances, to look out for coming storms and other disasters, and to both hunt prey and evade predators.

SEISMOLOGY

Yet another area where sound is put to use is in the field of seismology—the use of sound to map the interior of the Earth and to detect distant earthquakes. Geologists can both listen to seismic waves naturally caused by earthquakes and can generate their own—both techniques are important tools in the hands of qualified geologists.

An earthquake occurs when rock breaks to form a fault, or when rock slides along a fault line. The energy that is released from such an event can cause the entire Earth to ring like a bell. Using a sensitive detector, a large earthquake can be detected anywhere in the world. And because earthquakes generate two different kinds of waves (which act differently when passing through the Earth), these waves can be used to make an "X-ray" of the inside of the Earth.

One kind of wave is called a *p-wave*, a wave of pressure that acts just like sound waves traveling through air or water. In a p-wave, the molecules are briefly pushed closer together, and then relax again as the wave passes. P-waves travel through any substance and will travel to and from anywhere in the Earth. This is not true of the other kind of wave, which is known as the *s-wave*. S-waves are also called *shear waves* and are formed when materials shear, or slide on top of each other. One example of shearing is to put a deck of cards on the

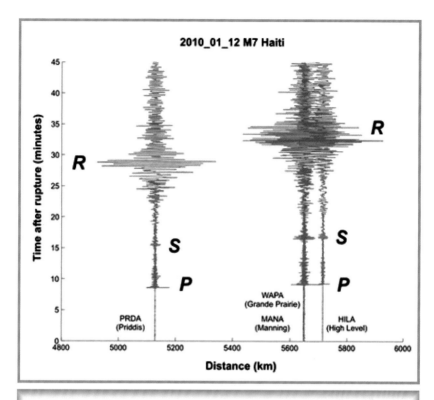

Figure 3.5 The January 2010 Haiti earthquake was recorded by seismograph machines in Canada. These seismographic recordings, taken from the Priddis, Grande Pairie, High Level, and Manning stations, show the primary (*P*) and secondary (*S*) waves, which followed a shorter path through the Earth's mantle, as well as Rayleigh (*R*) waves that propagate more slowly along the surface.

table, then put your hand on top of the top card and move your hand to the side—the top card sticks to your hand, the bottom card sticks to the table, and the cards in between slide across one another. The same thing happens when s-waves pass through rock.

What makes s-waves so revealing is that they pass through solids, but not through liquids (because liquids don't shear the way that solids do). Scientists noticed that after an earthquake some seismic stations "saw" p-waves but did not "see" s-waves. This observation eventually led them to only one explanation—parts of the Earth's interior are liquid, not solid. Decades of analysis have shown us that the Earth has many layers (all of which have been identified by using this seismic information). These layers consists of a solid inner core, a liquid outer core, a semi-solid mantle, a liquid asthenosphere (the layer that the continents slide around on), and a solid crust. Thanks to seismic stations located all over the world, not an earthquake goes unrecorded, often by multiple stations. The information these stations gather from quakes usually ends up online where anyone can make use of it.

Geologists who are mapping the layers of rock beneath a proposed drilling site in the search for gold or oil sometimes need to make their own "mini-earthquakes." To accomplish this, they set off an explosive charge that sends sound waves into the ground. The sound waves, in turn, reflect back from the layers of rock below, providing information about the composition of the rocks and the structure of the layers. With this data, geologists can make more

How Microphones Work

Anything that vibrates can produce sound, and the frequency of the sound is controlled by the speed of the vibration. A vibrating string can cause only a single family of sounds, depending on how rapidly it's vibrating. For more complex sounds, a more complicated setup is needed. A vibrating membrane (a sheet of plastic, for example) can create more complex vibrations, which can produce more complex sounds. And when vibrations strike the membrane, it will begin to vibrate as well. In a stereo system—in most speakers in fact—electrical signals cause a magnet to turn on and off rapidly. The vibrating magnetic field that results causes the speaker to vibrate. This works the other way, too—if a speaker membrane is made to vibrate while hooked up to a small magnet, the setup can be used to generate an electrical current. The electrical current can then be sent to a speaker located elsewhere where the process is reversed—this is how a telephone works.

informed guesses as to where minerals might have accumulated and recommend areas to explore.

Even when they are not used in the search for minerals, seismic surveys can convey important information. Seismic surveys helped uncover the hidden crater that was left by the huge meteor that struck the Earth millions of years ago, the effects of which may have caused the dinosaurs' extinction.

Light and Sound and the Senses

O ur world is suffused with light and sound. Virtually every multi-celled organism has developed senses to detect light and sound, and many organisms have developed ways to produce them as well. The ability to make sound is fairly common with organisms, much more common than the ability to make light, although there are creatures (fireflies, some jellyfish, and some deep-sea fish) that produce small amounts of light.

Yet, with the rare exceptions of animals that live deep underground and that have lost their sight, all living organisms can sense light (even scallops have eyes), and even animals without ears (such as snakes) can sense vibrations, including those that are caused by sound waves. Snakes may be deaf in that they may not be able to distinguish between different tones and sounds, but they can still sense noise. For that matter, many deaf humans can dance by keeping time with the music vibrations they can feel from the thumping drums or bass notes. Now we will explain how animals sense light and sound, how the ears and eyes work, as well as other ways of sensing phenomena.

HOW THE EYES SENSE LIGHT

The human eye (and the eyes of most mammals and birds for that matter) is similar to a camera: Light passes through a clear protective covering (the **cornea**) to enter the eye, and then passes through a small aperture (the **iris**) to enter the eye itself. Inside the eye and behind the iris is a small lens. Just as with a camera lens, light is refracted and focused on the back of the eye. Finally, at the back of the eye is the **retina**, which plays the same role as film (in a non-digital camera) or a light-sensing CCD chip (in a digital camera). The retina is filled with cells that detect the focused image, transform that into nerve impulses, and shoot the information off to the brain through the **optic nerve**. The brain is where the image is formed—not in the eye. The eye is simply a light detector (a sophisticated one, to be sure), and the brain is where "seeing" takes place. The following paragraph explains how this works.

Think about how a camera operates: The lens focuses light, but it certainly cannot see. The film (or CCD) is made up of a lot of tiny areas that sense light (such as grains of light-sensing material in film and individual electronic "wells" in a CCD chip). Any one of these areas can detect light, but each one only senses a very tiny bit of the entire image. So, no single well and no single grain of film can "see" the entire picture—all that they can detect is how much light falls on that particular tiny bit of the image. Therefore, "seeing" cannot take place with the film either—the film is just a collection of information, but it can't ascribe meaning to the information it has recorded. Our eyes work in the same way—every single cell of the retina acts like a single CCD well (or a single grain of film). It is only able to record the number of photons (particles of light) that fall on it. Therefore, a single cell in our retina can only tell us how much light it detected—it certainly can't tell us what its neighbors detect. So, like a camera, the retina can only detect light—it can only collect this information—but it can't put this information together to make a picture. That's where the brain comes into play.

The optic nerve is a bundle of nerve fibers that goes directly from the retina to the brain. Every single light receptor cell in the eye has its own nerve, and every nerve is attached to a specific cell in the brain. This is an important fact—every single light-detecting cell in the retina is in direct communication with a single cell in the brain. When light strikes the retina, that information goes directly to the brain and "lights up" a corresponding cell in the visual part of our brain. In effect, there is a virtual replica of our retina in our brain

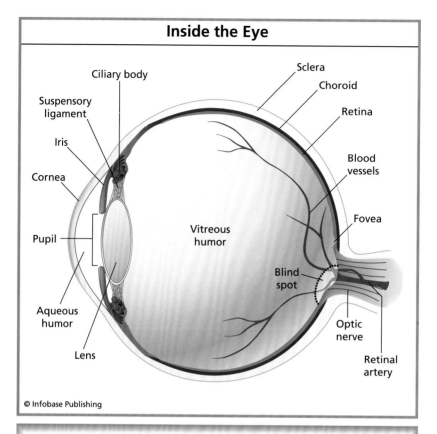

Inside the Eye

Ciliary body

Suspensory
ligament

Iris

Cornea

Pupil

Aqueous
humor

Lens

Sclera

Choroid

Retina

Blood
vessels

Fovea

Vitreous
humor

Blind
spot

Optic
nerve

Retinal
artery

© Infobase Publishing

Figure 4.1 The cornea and lens focus light rays onto the fovea, the part of the retina that has the highest density of cones. When light is focused directly on the optic nerve, called the blind spot, a person cannot see the light. Because human eyes have overlapping fields of view and the human brain can fill in missing details, people don't see any interruptions or gaps in images.

tissue. This visual part of the brain scans these cells (which make up the virtual retina) to record what each of them is sensing. When this process is completed, an image finally forms. Only then, have we truly "seen" what we are looking at. Remember, the information collected by the eye is only information; it does not become an image until the brain collects that information and puts it all together into a coherent picture.

Now it's time to go back and look at some of the other things happening inside the eye to help make sense of a little more of what is going on. In particular, the way that the lens and the retina work is fascinating and is worth reviewing in a little more detail.

One of the aspects of the eye that was mentioned earlier is that the lens focuses light, in the same way that a camera lens (or the lens of a microscope or telescope) focuses light. But it might be helpful to explain what it means to **focus** something. The first thing to realize is that the world we are looking at is a lot bigger than the inside of our eyes. This may seem obvious, but it also means that we need to have some way of compressing a view of the entire outdoors into an area the size of an eyeball. This means bending the rays of light so that, say, the image of a house can fit onto a retina that's only an inch or so across. Not only that, but the image has to be sharp—we can't just bend light rays willy-nilly; they have to be bent and brought together clearly, as shown in the picture. This is what *focus* means—first, that rays of light are bent to bring them together into a smaller image and, second, that the resulting image is clear and sharp. What this second part means is that the rays of light coming from, say, the tip of a pencil and the rays of light coming from the eraser at the pencil's other end all end up at the same point on the retina. If there are defects in the lens, some of the light rays may up in one spot, while some of them end up in another—this will result in a smeared-out image that is fuzzy and difficult to discern.

Thus, the lens focuses images on the back of the eye, but that image still has to be registered and transmitted to the brain. This is where the retina comes in. The retina is made of specialized cells that can detect light. What's interesting is that our retinas have two different kinds of light-detecting cells; they are called **rods** and **cones**. Cones, which help us to see colors, are concentrated in the central part of the retina. Each human eye has about 6 million cones, which means that our color vision is similar to a 6 megapixel digital camera. The rods only detect black and white and work best at night because they are very sensitive to low levels of light. There are about 125 million rods located throughout the entire retina, but most of them are concentrated in the retina's outer parts. For this reason, the rods also give us much of our peripheral vision. In fact, it is sometimes easier to see things by using our peripheral vision at night or in very dim light.

When light hits these light-detecting cells, it deposits energy into the cells' molecules, causing chemical changes. The cells register

Rods and Cones in the Retina

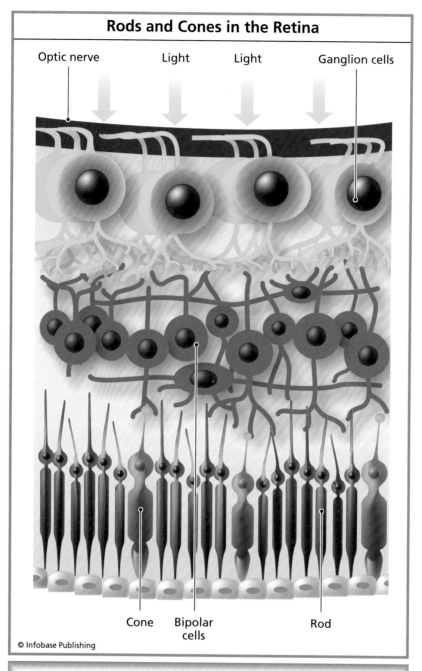

Optic nerve   Light   Light   Ganglion cells

Cone   Bipolar   Rod
cells

© Infobase Publishing

Figure 4.2 The retina consists of a large number of cells, including rod and cone photoreceptors at the back of the eye. Cells process the signals from photoreceptors and send the findings to the visual part of the brain via the optic nerve. Light passes through the transparent layers of cells before being intercepted by photoreceptors.

these chemical changes and give off small electrical impulses that travel along the optic nerves to the brain, where they activate the corresponding cells in the visual cortex. From this, we can understand that the retina is really not so much like film (which can only record an image once), but is more like a digital camera's CCD chip—it continually records information and passes it on to the brain.

Of course, not all animal eyes are like the human eye. Most mammals' eyes are like ours, as are most birds' eyes. But cephalopods (such as squid, octopi, and their relatives) have eyes that are just as sophisticated as ours—but they are different. The biggest difference between humans and cephalopods is that, in our eyes, the retina is inverted—the light-sensing cells are located on the back of the retina, so light has to pass through the retina to reach them. One of the results of the way our retina is designed is that we have a blind spot—we can't see in the place where the optic nerve enters the retina because that nerve takes the place of the light-sensing cells.

A squid, however, has no blind spot—its retina has the light-sensing cells on the front of the retina, including over the top of the optic nerve. Interestingly, this also means that cephalopods' eyes evolved independently of mammals, birds, and other organisms that have eyes like ours. Like flight (which evolved independently in birds, insects, and mammals), vision is so important that it has evolved in several directions throughout the history of life.

Other animal species—all kinds of insects, fish, and reptiles—have even more different kinds of eyes. The simplest kind of eye is a simple patch of cells that is sensitive to light; this sort of an eye can't form an image, but it can tell the difference between day and night, and can alert an animal to danger. (That large shadow blocking out the Sun may be a hungry predator.) To make it more complex, putting these cells in the bottom of a small pit in the animal's body makes for a slightly more effective eye that helps the animal know what direction the light is coming from (meaning whichever way the pit is facing). Narrowing the opening of the pit (while widening the pit itself) creates the equivalent of a pinhole camera—an eye that can form an image, although not a very sharp one (for example, one cephalopod, called the chambered nautilus, has a pinhole eye). The next advancement is to form a lens to help focus light. Eyes that use lenses are found in insects, fish, amphibians, reptiles, birds, and mammals.

What is important to remember is that, in spite of the great differences between all of the eyes in these animals, there are also some remarkable similarities. Every eye contains cells that are sensitive to light. Every animal has a way to pass information from its eyes to its brain (or for simpler animals such as jellyfish, its nervous system), which can then interpret whatever signals are transmitted. These fundamental similarities are even more important when we remember the number of times that eyes have evolved throughout history and how widely they are distributed throughout the animal kingdom—to be able to see is so important and, because of the properties that light has, there are only so many ways that it can be captured and used. The design of our eyes, and the design of every other eye in nature, is dictated by the physics and the properties of light.

HOW THE EARS SENSE SOUND AND THE VOICE PRODUCES SOUND

Sound vibrations travel through air, water, rock, and soil—in fact, through any substance (although some substances conduct sound better than others). Any object that is in contact with the ground, or immersed in the water or air, will be exposed to these vibrations. Anything that can feel pressure will be able to feel these vibrations, as long as the vibrations are strong enough to be felt. This is how a snake, for example, is able to sense when a hiker is drawing near. The hiker's footsteps produce vibrations that are transmitted through the ground and into the snake's body.

However, snakes can't hear sounds; they can only feel vibrations. Humans can sense sonic vibrations, too. People who stand in front of a speaker when the stereo is playing loudly will feel the thump of the bass through their bodies. But what turns vibrations into sounds are the ears.

Ears work pretty much the same way as microphones: Sound vibrations in the air cause the eardrum (a thin membrane of tissue) to start vibrating. Attached to the eardrum are three small bones—the hammer, anvil, and stirrup (or, in Latin, the *malleus, incus,* and *stapes*), which vibrate along with the eardrum. These bones, in turn, are attached to a snail-shaped structure in the inner ear—the **cochlea**—which is filled with fluid and cells with small hairs growing out of them. These hairs are sensitive to different pitches (frequencies) of sound; when the vibrations pass through the fluid they cause the hairs to vibrate, which activates nerve cells that, in turn, pass the information on to our brains, with the result that we hear that particular frequency. Real sound is composed of a wide range of frequencies, so many cells are activated and we hear a medley of frequencies.

Our ears also reveal clues to our evolutionary heritage. Our outer ears show that we live immersed in air. If we lived in the water, we'd have no need for an outer ear. From studying the bones in our ears, we know that these bones vibrate best at frequencies that travel easily through the air. What is even more interesting is where the bones themselves came from and what that tells us about our history.

Feel along your lower jaw and notice how your jawbone ends just below your ears. What is interesting about this is that the bones in our ears used to be part of the jaw of our ancestors. Fish and reptiles both have simpler ears than we have, and they both have more complicated jawbones than humans—they have more bones in their jaws, in fact, than the single bone that mammals have. Hard as it may be to believe, the small bones at the end of the reptilian and fish jaws have, through the ages, moved to the insides of our heads where we now use them to hear. One of our ear bones came from a distant fish ancestor, while the other two came from the reptilian jaw. Amazingly, we can read several hundred million years of our evolutionary heritage in the way that we hear sounds.

There are other ways of making ears. Some amphibians have tympanic membranes—that's like having an eardrum on the outside of their heads. Some insects also have tympanic membranes (even, in some cases, located on their legs), which is how they hear the chirps and clicks of other insects. Yet, insects that don't have tympanic membranes can still sense sounds with hairs located on their legs or elsewhere on their bodies: They may not hear the same sounds that we do, but they presumably hear them, instead of feeling only vibrations.

Yet, animals not only do more than hear sounds, they produce them too. Virtually every form of life more complicated than jellyfish can produce sounds. Insects make sounds by rubbing their wings together or against their legs, or by rubbing their legs together. All of these make sound pretty much the same way that a stringed instrument does—by making the wings or legs vibrate.

Inside the Ear

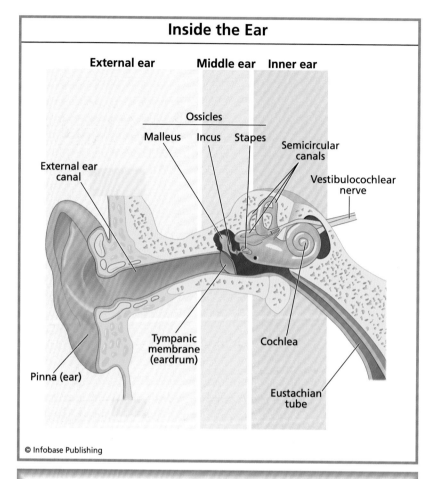

External ear   **Middle ear**   **Inner ear**

Ossicles

Malleus   Incus   Stapes

Semicircular
canals

External ear
canal

Vestibulocochlear
nerve

Tympanic
membrane
(eardrum)

Cochlea

Pinna (ear)

Eustachian
tube

Figure 4.3   The outer ear funnels sound waves into the external ear canal. The three tiny bones of the middle ear (the ossicles) act as a lever system, raising the pressure exerted on the oval window—the place where the inner ear begins. The inner ear includes the cochlea, which turns pressure waves into electrical signals that allow people to perceive sound.

And, truth be told, the way that they make sound is not terribly different in principle, even though the biology and the mechanism are a bit different.

Most mammals, including humans, have a larynx—a voice box—and how mammals make sounds has a lot in common with the way a musical instrument makes sound. The human larynx contains vocal folds. (Scientists call them vocal folds because they are small flaps

Figure 4.4 This male great green bush cricket is in calling position. Crickets produce sound by rubbing specific parts of their wings together. At the base of their forewing, a thick, rigid vein acts as a file, while the upper surface of the forewing is hard, like a scraper. When rubbed together, the thin portions of the wings vibrate and amplify the sound being made.

of tissue that are stretched across the trachea that carries air to our lungs.) Whenever we talk or sing, we make our vocal cords vibrate as we blow air past them—like the reed in a clarinet or oboe, or like a

Protecting Your Senses

Our eyes and ears are obviously important. Without our eyes, we cannot see. Without our vision, we cannot read, watch television and movies, drive cars, or play sports and video games. Many people around the world are blind, and they are at a disadvantage in a world that is run largely by those who can see. It makes sense to take care of our eyes.

The best way to do this is to avoid things that can hurt our eyes and to remember to wear safety glasses or goggles whenever we find ourselves, say, working in a laboratory, running a power saw or lathe, and doing other things that can send chemicals or splinters flying into our eyes. You may find yourself in plenty of circumstances where you have to wear safety glasses—and no matter how uncomfortable they are, and no matter how ugly they might be (although modern safety glasses don't look too bad), you must wear them.

The same precautions apply to our ears. Once we lose our hearing, we can't listen to music anymore, can't hear our friends or family talking with us, can't hear the TV or radio, and can never again enjoy the sounds of birds, the falling rain, or any of the other sounds of nature. Not only that, but we lose access to valuable information—you're more likely, for example, to be run over by a car if you can't hear it honk its horn at you.

One way to hurt your ears is by putting objects into the outer ear. If you put a pencil or pen in your ear and someone accidentally bumps your elbow, the pencil could wind up being jammed through your eardrum. This does more than harm your hearing—it hurts. Another way to hurt your ears is with sound that is too loud: Loud noise trumpeter buzzing their lips inside a mouthpiece. Again like a musical instrument, this buzzing is modified by the "pipe" the vocal cords are located in. The length of the vocal cords controls the sound that

can destroy the hair cells in your inner ear. These hairs do not regrow; once they are gone, there is no way to recover those frequencies that were picked up by the hairs. Our ears are wonderfully resistant organs, but they can still be damaged. Listening to music is still okay, even when it's loud—but only up to a point. It's the amount of loud music you listen to every day that matters; too much of it can cause too much damage that our ears won't be able to repair. The worst thing we can do for our hearing is to put headphones on and crank up the sound to the maximum. The next worst thing is to ride in a car with the sound system cranked up too high.

Being in a loud factory for too long can ruin your hearing, as can spending too much time near a loud engine, such as a jet or diesel. In situations like this, you should always be sure to take steps to protect your hearing. Like safety glasses, hearing protection, like ear plugs and ear muffs, can be uncomfortable to wear. But when you consider how much you enjoy listening to music and talking with your friends and family, it's more than worth the trouble to take the time to save your hearing for the things that matter to you.

One thing to remember when you're trying to decide whether or not you should wear safety glasses or hearing protection is that once you lose your eyesight or hearing, it's permanent. Spend a day with your ears plugged up and see how different everything is; spend a day going around your home with your eyes closed or wearing a blindfold and see what you miss. And remember that wearing protective gear and taking protective actions is only a temporary discomfort: If you don't use them when you need them, the effects may well last forever.

they can make, as do the length and diameter of our throats. Even the sinus cavities in our heads contribute to the sounds that come out of our mouths; the sound resonates inside these sinuses the same as it resonates within the body of a guitar or violin. Men tend to have longer and thicker vocal folds and so will tend to produce a deeper and more resonant voice than women. (Boys' voices deepen as they reach maturity.)

Extending the Senses

Humans can see only a tiny part of the electromagnetic spectrum: The rest of it is invisible to us. Similarly, humans can only hear a small part of the sonic spectrum: The rest of that is inaudible to us. We can't see objects much smaller than a human hair with the naked eye, and we can't see the whole of any object that is too large (for example, planet Earth as we're standing on it). Our senses are limited but we nevertheless live in a universe that is full of things that we cannot see or hear because of these limitations. To explore those parts of the universe that we can't see, we have to use technology to extend our senses. Microscopes and telescopes help us to see the invisibly small and the invisibly faint and distant and, to see in wavelengths that are invisible to our eyes, while other technologies have been developed to help us hear in frequencies that are beyond the range of our ears.

DEVELOPING METHODS TO "SEE" THE INVISIBLE

Earlier, we noted that lenses have been used by people since they were first developed for use as magnifying glasses thousands of years ago. For millennia, people have been using lenses to help make the tiny things of our world visible. With time, people also learned that they could use lenses in the form of **telescopes** to see further into the distance and that combining lenses would bring clearer images of the faraway objects at which they were looking. The telescope brought distant objects, in a sense, nearer to us and, as more powerful telescopes became available, we became able to see even more distant and fainter objects.

Telescopes work in two ways: First, they collect light, and second, they focus it. This may sound pretty mundane, but there's more to both of these properties of telescopes than one might think. First, we'll discuss the easy one: light collecting.

Astronomers have referred to telescopes as "light buckets" because their main purpose is to collect as much light as possible, in the way a bucket is used to collect water. Think of it this way: A star (for example) sends out light in all directions, but our eyes are very small—the iris (the opening that lets light into our eyes) is only a centimeter or so across, with an area of just a few square centimeters. Because of its size, the iris can absorb only so many photons from a dim object (just as putting a small glass out in a rainstorm can only capture a small amount of water). The way to catch more photons—to make a dim object visible—is to put out a huge bucket. Like a funnel, a telescope with a 33-foot-tall (10-m) mirror can catch more photons, funneling them into a point. This is part of what it takes for a telescope to make dim objects visible. But there's more—telescopes can also hold their focus for minutes, hours, or even days. This ability lets them collect even more photons and, therefore, to see even dimmer objects.

Our eyes collect photons for a fraction of a second and then pass that information on to the brain. Any information—in this case, the number of photons collected by each rod or cone—collected by the eye is passed on to the brain about 30 times each second. Yet, very few photons coming from a very dim object, like a distant galaxy, may even reach the Earth. It's likely that there may not be enough photons from such distant objects to hit any single cell in our eyes and register with the brain in a thirtieth of a second. However, a telescope can sit patiently and unblinkingly collect photons and focus them onto a small CCD chip (or piece of film) for hours. Again, like that glass left out in the rain, if you turn a telescope off after only a minute, it will not have collected nearly as much light inside it as when you leave it on for an hour. This is one way that telescopes enable us to see the invisible—by collecting more photons for a longer time than is possible through our biological eyes alone.

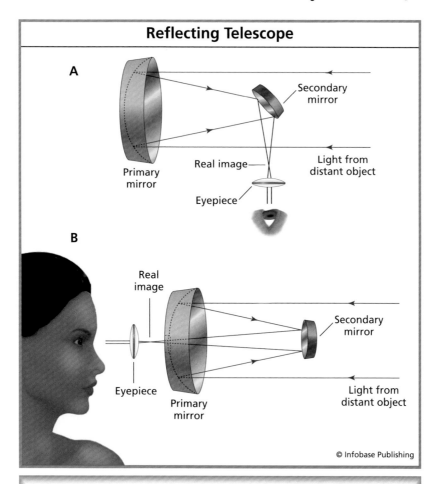

Reflecting Telescope

A

Secondary mirror

Real image

Light from distant object

Primary mirror

Eyepiece

B

Real image

Secondary mirror

Eyepiece

Light from distant object

Primary mirror

© Infobase Publishing

Figure 5.1 The mirror of a reflecting telescope focuses light, which is directed either to the side (a) or out a primary mirror (b).

Even if light-collecting was all that telescopes could do, they would still be incredibly valuable instruments. Yet, in fact, they can do more, making them even more valuable.

Now, consider how a magnifying lens works. As an object gives off light in all directions, some of that light takes a direct path to our eyes while some of it doesn't. With the help of a lens or a mirror, some of those diverging rays of light that would otherwise miss our eyes can be bent by the lens so that when we put our eyes at the lens's focus, the distant object looks larger than it would otherwise.

In this way, a telescope can make something in the distance appear to be large enough to see.

Most optical devices use a number of lenses in combination—these are called compound lenses. These particular lenses are used to correct what is called chromatic aberration. Different colors have different wavelengths and the colors tend to separate as they pass through a lens (this is how a prism creates a rainbow from simple sunlight). This chromatic aberration happens with camera and telescope lenses as well, so lens makers will put in a second lens element—called an achromatic lens—that brings these divergent colors back together again. Most optical devices—cameras, binoculars, telescopes, microscopes, and more—use compound lenses because a single lens, while helpful, can only accomplish so much.

Telescopes can bring us within view of the invisibly far, and microscopes use much of the same principle to show us the invisibly small. But while ordinary telescopes and microscopes see the visible light given off by objects, there is still much to see that remains invisible to us. Luckily, science has shown us how to bring the invisible into view as well. Today, scientists can "see" everything from radio waves to gamma rays, and the universe that is revealed by these wavelengths is a mind-blowing place. As any astronomer can tell us, visible light is not the only place where exciting things are happening. Now it's time to find out how we can see in other wavelengths, starting with longer wavelengths such as radio.

One thing to realize before we continue is that there is a very good reason that we see in visible light: There are only a few portions of the whole electromagnetic spectrum that can reach the surface of the Earth—visible light, radio waves, and some ultraviolet light. Radio waves are hard to detect and that is best accomplished by using long metal wires or large metal dishes that act as antennas. Not only was it easier for nature to develop small non-metallic things like eyes, but the Sun emits far more visible light than it does radio waves—the Sun is brighter in those wavelengths.

Infrared Rays

The first stop in our journey through the long-wavelength side of the spectrum is infrared, or thermal radiation. Infrared doesn't penetrate the atmosphere very well, so the best way to look for it is to put a telescope where the atmosphere is thin and dry or to send it into outer space. Whatever way is chosen, once the telescope is in place, infrared can be focused pretty much the same as visible light—it is not so far away in wavelength as to render ordinary lenses and telescopes useless. Infrared shows us, for example, areas where warm dust is collecting around a star, a zone that might someday be found to host a planet like Earth or Mars.

Radio Waves

Radio waves are the next stop on the long-wavelength side of the spectrum. Humans use radio waves to broadcast television and radio signals. Microwaves are a high-frequency form of radio wave and they are used for microwave ovens, cell phone signals, and wireless Internet. Higher radio frequencies are used for radar. Even on Earth, radar helps us to see things that may be beyond the view of a telescope. Radio waves can also penetrate clouds and dust, so even an overcast sky is transparent to radar.

In space, the radio sky is tremendously different from what the naked eye can see. Radio waves are given off mostly by fast-moving charged particles (usually electrons) speeding up or slowing down, or they are being bent by magnetic fields. Radio waves are also emitted by some atoms or molecules. Hydrogen, for example, emits radio-frequency radiation at a wavelength of 21 centimeters, so mapping the sky at this wavelength can help astronomers locate clouds of hydrogen and areas where stars may one day form. But radio waves also show where exciting events in the universe have already taken place.

Some of the largest—and most exciting—objects in the universe are visible only when viewed in radio wavelengths. For example, huge "radio lobes" can be detected on opposite sides of some galaxies. These lobes may have formed when two galaxies collided, subsequently creating a super-massive **black hole**, which can weigh a billion times as much as the Sun, in the center of the galaxy. (A black hole is typically a collapsed star that is so massive and so dense that it has a tremendously high gravitational field from which not even light can escape.) A black hole blasts jets of hot gas thousands or even millions of light-years into space. The protons and electrons it contains circle frantically around magnetic lines of force, emitting radio waves that can be seen from across the universe by radio telescopes.

Figure 5.2 The supermassive black hole at the center of the Milky Way is known as Sagittarius A* (or Sgr A*, for short).

Quasars

Some of the objects first found through the use of radio wavelengths are among the brightest and most distant things in the universe: **quasars**. The word *quasar* stands for quasi-stellar radio source; quasi-stellar means that they are so small that they look like points of light (just like stars do).

Quasars shine brightly in radio wavelengths. It was easy for astronomers to determine that quasars were objects located far away. In fact, the Doppler shift (explained in the next paragraph) of the radio waves showed these objects to be billions of light-years away.

Still, for years, astronomers had no idea how such a distant object could be so bright in terms of radio wavelengths and had no idea how quasars worked. Eventually, they realized that quasars were very young galaxies with black holes at their centers, still collecting gas and dust. Active black holes give off a lot of energy, and much of this energy goes into making light and blasting jets of gas into the space between the galaxies.

We now have a picture of what the sky looks like when seen in radio wavelengths: a realm of furious activity containing huge lobes of gas filled with spiraling electrons and protons that show us the locations of galaxies in which active, super-massive black holes spin at their centers while clouds of hydrogen gas—possibly the birthplaces of future stars—float in space.

The **Doppler effect** helps astronomers understand a lot of what is going on in the universe. We experience the Doppler effect when an ambulance siren sounds higher-pitched as it approaches and then switches to a lower-pitch when it passes by. As the ambulance is approaching, the sound waves are crammed together, thereby raising the frequency. As the ambulance speeds away in the other direction, the sound waves become stretched out into a lower tone. By using fairly precise measurements and by knowing the frequency of the siren's sound when it is not moving, a scientist can calculate exactly how fast the ambulance is moving toward or away from an observer.

Light acts in the same way. A light that is moving toward Earth from a faraway object will be a bluer color (because the wavelengths are crammed closer together), while reddened light means that an object is moving away. As shown with the ambulance, the exact speed of the object can be calculated when the precise wavelength of the original light is compared with the red-shifted light that astronomers see in the sky.

X-ray and Gamma Ray Astronomy

As previously discussed, hotter objects give off shorter-wavelength light. X-rays emit some of the shortest wavelengths, and they mark the location of the hottest objects in the universe (gamma rays are something else entirely—more about them a little later). X-rays, for example, mark the spot where matter vanishes from the universe

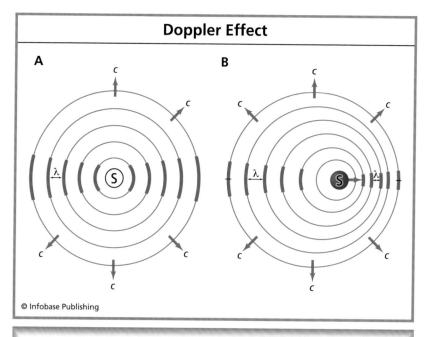

Figure 5.3   In (a), you can see a stationary sound source, called S, emitting sound waves that spread out in all directions and have the same wavelength. In (b), a sound source is shown moving to the right. To a stationary observer, the sound waves in front of the source are bunched up and have a shorter wavelength than the sound waves behind the source.

into black holes. X-rays also reveal to us the presence of vast clouds of million-degree gas in the space between the galaxies, and they show us the remnants of stars that exploded millions of years in the past. Bright spots in the X-ray sky reveal to us sites of unimaginable violence in the universe.

X-rays, however, cannot penetrate the atmosphere. There is no way to see them from the Earth's surface. Our own use of X-ray vision began when X-ray telescopes were floated up into the stratosphere on balloons, and has continued with the launch of Uhuru, the first orbital X-ray observatory. One of the most recent X-ray telescopes, Chandra, was sent into orbit in 1999, right before the beginning of the twenty-first century. Since then, it has taken some of the most detailed pictures yet of the universe using X-rays.

Figure 5.4 This X-ray image of M51, the Whirlpool Galaxy, was taken by Chandra.

Black holes contain the strongest gravity in the universe; no matter or energy that falls into a black hole can escape. Just as water swirls around before vanishing down the drain, matter swirls into a black hole and accumulates into a disk of gas and dust (called an accretion disk) that orbits the black hole. Matter falls onto the accretion disk at nearly the speed of light. Most of the matter's kinetic energy is turned into heat, reaching temperatures of millions of degrees. Matter this hot doesn't give off yellow or red light, but glows with the light of X-rays.

X-rays also mark the locations of stars that have died. Late in their lives, many stars blow their outer layers off into space, forming rings of gas and dust that are called planetary nebulae. Later, when these stars die, they are blown apart and the debris is blasted into space. When this debris plows into the planetary nebulae, the gas

The Chandra X-ray Observatory

Visible light can be focused with lenses. In the few thousand years since lenses were first invented, humans have become very good at making them. Yet X-rays zip right through glass without even stopping, and so glass can't focus X-rays. To make an X-ray telescope, a different approach has to be taken.

The Chandra X-ray Observatory uses what is called a grazing-incidence mirror to focus X-rays onto their detectors. This mirror looks like nothing more than a bunch of smooth metal barrels, nested inside of each other like a set of Russian dolls. Although X-rays can pass right through metal if they strike it at a high angle, things are different if they come in at a very low angle; instead of passing through or being absorbed by the metal, an X-ray will just barely graze the surface and reflect very slightly toward the center of the barrels. Chandra has two sets of these mirrors, all of them machined and polished to incredibly close tolerances—some of the smoothest surfaces ever made. With these, Chandra has been able to take the most detailed X-ray photos to date of the X-ray universe.

heats up to millions of degrees and gives off X-rays. Supernova remnants are laced with tendrils of X-ray emissions.

The other place in the universe where X-rays can be detected is in the space between the galaxies. Intergalactic space is very nearly the emptiest part of the universe, but it still contains tremendous amounts of gas. This gas can reach temperatures of millions of degrees, hot enough to give off X-rays and form a sort of X-ray fog that fills billions of cubic light-years of space.

Unlike X-rays, the presence of gamma rays does not always mean the presence of incredibly hot matter. Gamma rays are nothing more than higher-energy versions of X-rays. However, it's where gamma rays *come from* that make the difference. Gamma rays are usually given off by radioactive elements in the universe, and many radioactive elements are produced in exploding stars. Some supernovae, for example, produce a "solar mass" of radioactive nickel (meaning that the radioactive nickel alone weighs as much as the Sun). This nickel gives off gamma radiation, as does the radioactive cobalt that it forms when it decays. Radioactive aluminum is also ejected into space during these explosions.

By mapping the sky in gamma rays, we can see the tombs of former stars. But, beginning in the 1960s, gamma ray satellites put up to detect nuclear weapons explosions made an even more intriguing discovery—one that shocked scientists when they finally understood what they were seeing.

About once a day, somewhere in the visible universe, a powerful burst of gamma rays appears, seemingly out of nowhere, shines for a few seconds, and then vanishes. For over 30 years, gamma ray bursts puzzled the scientific community. For much of that time, scientists didn't even know from how far away the bursts were coming. Some scientists thought they might originate in the distant suburbs of our own solar system, while others thought they might reside in our galaxy, and still others felt that they must be billions of light-years away. Until a flash could be seen in visible light, however, the question of what these **gamma ray bursts** were remained open.

In the late 1990s, astronomers discovered that gamma ray bursts were coming from all over the sky. This at least showed that they were not in our own solar system or in our galaxy but, instead, scattered about the universe. Finally, in 1998, a visual counterpart was finally found, and astronomers realized that gamma ray bursts originate from incredible distances of billions of light-years away, as far as halfway across the universe from our galaxy. At such great distances, it was realized, they must be incredibly powerful to be seen at all. In fact, gamma ray bursts are probably the most powerful explosions that have taken place in our universe since the Big Bang. The shorter gamma ray bursts might occur when two neutron stars coalesce into each other, and the longer ones might happen when the core of a huge star collapses into a black hole. Discovering, mapping, and learning the nature of gamma ray bursts is fascinating and important to understanding some of the most violent events in the universe.

When scientists look at the universe using visible light, they see an incredible array of beautiful sights everywhere. Yet, as wonderful as the visible universe is, the invisible universe is even more fantastic. Astronomers would never have known the half of it were they not able to extend our vision beyond visible light.

SOUND: NEW WAYS OF "HEARING" THE INAUDIBLE

Thanks to technology, scientists have found ways to extend human vision far beyond its ordinary abilities. Different technologies have provided the ability to do the same with sound. However, unlike light, sound can only travel through matter.

One way to extend the sense of hearing is by developing devices to listen to sounds that are too faint for the ears. One device is known as a parabolic microphone, a microphone that uses a curved dish to focus sounds the same way that a telescope mirror focuses light. These microphones are often seen on the sidelines of football games, where technicians aim them at players to enable television viewers to hear close-up the action on the field, almost as if they were actually with the players. They are also used by both police and private investigators (and spies, too, for that matter) to eavesdrop on private conversations. Another form of eavesdropping can only be used in rooms with windows, where sound waves from conversations can cause the window glass to vibrate ever so slightly. These vibrations can be "read" with a laser reflected from the window.

Table 5.1: Radiation and Its Uses

Type of radiation	Wavelength	Natural phenomena	Human uses
Gamma rays	< 0.1 nm	Radioactive decay, gamma ray bursts, matter-antimatter annihilation	Cancer therapy, nuclear medicine, non-destructive testing
X-rays	0.1–10 nm	Very hot gas (very hot interstellar gas, supernovae debris, black holes, neutron stars)	Medical diagnosis, luggage inspections, art authentication, cancer therapy
Ultraviolet	~10–400 nm	Hot gas (stars, somewhat cooler interstellar gas, damage—sunburn—to plants and animals)	Sterilization, "grow lights" for plants, curing polymers
Visible light	~400–600 nm	Stars, galaxies	Lasers, light bulbs, light-emitting diodes, etc.
Infrared	10,000 nm–100 microns	Warm interstellar gas and dust	Heat lamps, TV and stereo remote control units
Terahertz radiation and sub-millimeter radiation	~100 microns –1 mm	Star formation, warm dust and gas clouds	Security scans, medical imaging
Microwave and radio frequency	mm and longer wavelength	Radio galaxies	Radar, cooking, communications

These are only a few of the techniques that people have found to listen in on each other, even at distances that are too great for normal hearing. Another way to hear sounds at great distances, in this case underwater, involves the use of sensitive microphones called hydrophones (see the sidebar for more information).

In moving beyond what is audible to the human ear, engineers and scientists have found ways to hear and to use inaudible frequencies, just as they have found ways to help us to see at invisible wavelengths. Earlier, we talked about infrasound and ultrasound. Now it's time to learn a little more about them.

Ultrasound turns out to be a surprisingly useful tool (although high-frequency sound doesn't always travel far enough to be useful for long-distance work). Ultrasound is defined as sound beyond the range of human hearing. Interestingly, there are many animals that are not as limited in what they can hear as humans are. Therefore, sounds that would be considered "ultrasound" to humans are easily audible to these animals. Bats and dolphins, for example, use ultrasound to navigate. (Specially designed microphones provide a lot of information about the sounds they make.) In addition, dogs, mice, and cats can hear ultrasound frequencies.

In the case of ultrasound, the vibration frequency is at least 20,000 vibrations per second. Interestingly, experiments have shown that the human brain does show awareness of ultrasonic frequencies, even if the frequencies are not consciously heard. Normally, ultrahigh frequencies are filtered out by the bones of the middle ear so they're unable to reach the inner ear. But when the middle ear is bypassed, usually by introducing the vibrations directly into the bones of the head, the vibrations can be sensed by the cochlea. Test subjects were not consciously aware of the high frequencies, but their brain waves made it clear that they heard them. When scientists want to hear ultrasound, they have to first record the high-pitched sounds and then lower the frequency for playback—effectively like slowing down a tape recorder.

To make and listen to ultrasound requires a piece of equipment called a **transducer**. Technically, a transducer is any device that can change one sort of energy into another. In the field of acoustics—the science of sound—a transducer is used to change electrical energy into acoustic energy, and vice versa.

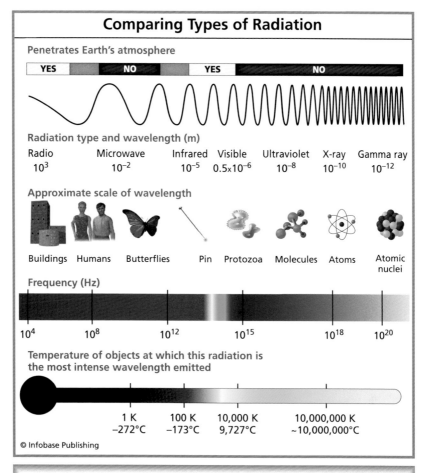

Comparing Types of Radiation

Penetrates Earth's atmosphere

| YES | NO | YES | NO |

Radiation type and wavelength (m)

| Radio | Microwave | Infrared | Visible | Ultraviolet | X-ray | Gamma ray |
| 10^3 | 10^{-2} | 10^{-5} | $0.5{\times}10^{-6}$ | 10^{-8} | 10^{-10} | 10^{-12} |

Approximate scale of wavelength

| Buildings | Humans | Butterflies | Pin | Protozoa | Molecules | Atoms | Atomic nuclei |

Frequency (Hz)

| 10^4 | 10^8 | 10^{12} | 10^{15} | 10^{18} | 10^{20} |

Temperature of objects at which this radiation is the most intense wavelength emitted

| 1 K | 100 K | 10,000 K | 10,000,000 K |
| −272°C | −173°C | 9,727°C | ~10,000,000°C |

© Infobase Publishing

Figure 5.5 Different kinds of wavelengths look and behave differently. This chart compares wavelengths' size, frequency, and abilities.

The most widely used kind of transducer for ultrasound employs a phenomenon called piezoelectricity (pronounced *pee-AY-zo electricity*). A piezoelectric crystal will produce electricity when it is made to vibrate, or it will vibrate when electricity flows through it. Therefore, by monitoring the electrical current the crystal produces, one can understand the nature of the ultrasonic vibrations that set it in motion.

Another area in which ultrasound can help is in finding locations. Although the Global Positioning System (GPS) is now used for navigation, it has some limitations. To achieve highly precise location measurements may require better approaches. The use of ultrasound provides one way to achieve this. For example, surveyors can set up ultrasound transducers at precise locations around sites that are being surveyed. Then, they can walk through the site with receivers and be able to determine their position very accurately by measuring it with respect to several ultrasound transmitters.

Infrasound

Infrasound—sound that is too low-pitched for humans to hear—is a little harder to work with. That's primarily because the very low frequencies can mean very long wavelengths, and long wavelengths

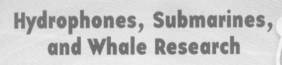

Hydrophones, Submarines, and Whale Research

Hydrophones are underwater microphones. They are transducers, small devices that turn electrical impulses into sound and vice versa. Submarines use lots of hydrophones—on some subs, a 15-foot (4.5-m) diameter sphere studded with them is placed at the front of the sub. A submarine also can trail a half-mile (0.8-km) long cable behind it that is also covered with hydrophones. Submarines depend on their hydrophones for the same reason whales do: Light only penetrates so far into the water. The only way to "see" more than a few hundred yards in any direction, or more than a few hundred feet deep underwater is with sound.

While submarines can use "active sonar"—broadcasting sound waves—to detect their surroundings, they mostly use their hydrophones to listen ("passive sonar") with incredible sensitivity. It is not unusual for a submarine to track the movements of another ship (submerged or on the surface) to distances of 20 miles (32 km) or more. If the other ship is noisy enough and sea conditions are good, a ship can be heard and tracked from more than 50 miles necessitate the use of large devices to both produce and record the sounds. In fact, humans do not normally produce infrasound because it is neither as useful (yet) nor as easy to produce as ultrasound. Infrasound is mostly used for scientific research. In addition, many large animals seem to use it to communicate. Elephants, for example, seem able to communicate up to two or three miles (3–4.8 km)by making infrasound noises; studying elephants' sounds teaches us more about them.

Yet, infrasound is even more valuable in understanding the physical world; many weather phenomena produce infrasound, and it may be possible someday to better predict when severe weather will strike by listening for the low-frequency sounds produced by wind

(80.5 km) away. (There are, however, plenty of stories of submarines drawn to within a quarter mile [0.4 km] of their quarry without being heard, and some advanced submarines actually create less noise than the ocean itself.)

Whales have their own version of sonar, both active and passive, using the biological equivalent of hydrophones. However, while submarines use the same hydrophones for transmitting and receiving, whales (and humans, for that matter) use different equipment for making noise and hearing the results. And, while people must use sophisticated computers to unravel the meaning of sounds coming through the water, whales have a much more sophisticated computer—their brains. For all our technology, whales are the true sonar masters—after all, they evolved sonar millions of years ago, and we just invented our version less than a century ago.

One problem with the high-power sonar that is used by the military, however, is that it can harm whales, just as humans can be harmed by exposure to high-intensity sounds. In 2008, the U.S. Supreme Court ruled against environmental groups and allowed the Navy to continue using sonar, citing the importance of military training.

blowing over the water or land, or thunder rumbling from a great distance. Long wavelengths can travel farther than shorter ones; the sound from the eruption of the volcano Krakatoa in Indonesia in the nineteenth-century circled the Earth several times before it finally faded out. In fact, it may one day be possible to hear storms coming when they are still hundreds or thousands of miles distant.

Sound frequencies that are slightly lower than human hearing can be detected with microphones. These sounds merely have to be played back at slightly higher speeds to make them audible to the human ear. Much lower-frequency sounds are not as easily "heard," but their effects can still be detected by changes in air pressure—remember that sound travels as a pressure wave—using a **barometer**. The sound of the Krakatoa volcano explosion was detected as it circled the world by noting pressure changes on the barometers in use at that time.

In addition, earthquake scientists can use seismographs to measure low-frequency vibrations in the earth as pressure waves pass beneath our feet. To date, this is the best-known use for infrasound—not to predict upcoming disasters, but to better understand them after the fact. It may be that, one day, scientists will be able to use them to predict earthquakes, volcanoes, and tsunamis.

Light and Sound
in the Universe

L ight fills the universe. Anyone looking at the sky on a clear night can see this with their eyes, and when technology extends human vision into other wavelengths, there is even more to see. In addition to the objects in the heavens—stars, galaxies, radio lobes, and accretion disks—the sky is filled with a dim microwave glow: This is the afterglow from the Big Bang, the beginning of the universe. For a simple example, turn on a television to a channel that is not broadcasting any programming, where the screen is filled with "snow." Believe it or not, a small percentage of that snow comes from the first photons (particles of light) that were released after the Big Bang, photons that have been traveling through space ever since. Hidden within this background radiation are major clues about the earliest days of the universe.

PROBING THE UNIVERSE WITH LIGHT

Between the galaxies lie vast clouds of gas. Some of these clouds can have as much mass as entire galaxies and can be even larger. These clouds are largely invisible. Astronomers can see right through them to galaxies located at even greater distances. Yet, because very specific wavelengths of light are absorbed by the gas in these clouds, scientists were eventually able to discover them. (Remember that we previously discussed how every element can absorb and emit radiation in very specific wavelengths. Keep that in mind as we'll come back to that in a moment.)

The universe is expanding. This fact was proven nearly a century ago when American astronomer Edwin Hubble noticed that galaxies are all moving away from the Earth, and the more distant the galaxy, the more rapid its speed. There is a mathematical relationship between speed and distance: Measuring how fast a galaxy is moving away, or receding, from the Earth can reveal how distant it is. One important thing to keep in mind is that, in the universe, speed and distance are related to each other. Speed can be determined by measuring the Doppler shift of light coming from a galaxy. With this last bit of information, an astronomer can tell how rapidly a galaxy is moving. This information can be combined with the galaxy's distance to measure the expansion of the universe.

Thus, basic physics can calculate the precise wavelength of light emitted by an atom of hydrogen, and astronomers can measure the precise wavelength of light from a star or galaxy as seen from Earth. This enables scientists to measure how quickly a distant star or galaxy is moving away from the Earth and, with that knowledge, its distance from us. The consensus among astronomers today is that the Hubble Constant (Hubble's initial value for the expansion rate, which astronomers use to make this calculation), also called the Hubble Parameter, is about 70 kilometers/second per mega-parsec (1 parsec is about 3.26 light-years or about 20 million million miles, and a mega-parsec is 1 million parsecs, abbreviated as Mpc). From this, we can calculate that a galaxy a million parsecs from us (about 3.26 million light-years away) is moving away from the Earth at a speed of 43.5 miles (70 kilometers) every second. The measurement can be read the opposite way, too: If light from a galaxy has a redshift velocity of 87 miles (140 km) per second, it means the galaxy is at a distance of 2 Mpc (about 7.52 million light-years away).

Now that we have an understanding of the relationship of speed and distance in the universe, we can use it to help understand more about some immense clouds of hydrogen sitting in intergalactic space. In the 1980s, astronomers began a careful examination of the light coming from quasars. Now that they knew that quasars were located at an immense distance from Earth, they were curious to

Figure 6.1 American astronomer Edwin Hubble proved the existence of galaxies other than the Milky Way. He also discovered that the degree of Doppler shift seen in the light spectra from other galaxies increased in proportion to each galaxy's distance from Earth. This theory is called Hubble's Law.

see what they were made of and how they came to burn so brightly. They were surprised to find, in addition to the emissions they expected to see, there were, strangely, places where the quasar light faded out. Looking more closely, they realized that this fading out was due to the absorption of the distant light by clouds of gas that lay between the quasars and the Earth. It was quickly realized, too, that the quasar's light could be used to probe the clouds to find out what they were made of and where in the universe they resided. It was no surprise to find that many of these clouds were also quite distant, or to learn that they were mostly made of hydrogen, since most of the visible matter in the universe is hydrogen. So finding huge amounts of hydrogen in intergalactic space was no surprise.

What was a surprise was to find not one set of absorption lines (an absorption line is a dark line where the hydrogen gas—or another element—has absorbed a specific wavelength of light), but a veritable forest of lines. Astronomers were shocked to find that there were multiple clouds between the Earth and distant quasars, no matter which direction they looked. In fact, these absorption lines quickly became known as the Lyman alpha "forest," and the gas clouds that caused this were called the Lyman alpha forest clouds. Lyman alpha refers to a specific hydrogen emission line, with a wavelength of 121.6 nm (a nanometer [nm] is one billionth of a meter or one millionth of a millimeter), one of a family of hydrogen emission lines in the ultraviolet part of the spectrum. A photon of this wavelength is emitted when the electron around a hydrogen atom drops to the lowest energy level from the one next higher up. In effect, astronomers can use quasars as distant lighthouses. Quasar beams help reveal not only the clouds that lie between the quasars and us, but also how far away they are. The light from objects at the edge of the observable universe can help scientists probe the contents of space.

ECHOES OF THE BIG BANG

Figuring out what the universe contains is indeed fascinating, but it's not the most amazing thing that light reveals about the universe. That honor has got to go to one remaining fossil of the Big Bang—the cosmic microwave background radiation mentioned earlier. Even more amazingly, by studying the microwave radiation, scientists can actually "hear" the sounds of the universe from when it was only a fraction of its current age. At the very largest scales of size and time, it turns out that light and sound converge. Before we explore any further, though, a little history.

For decades, scientists argued among themselves over how the universe began. The conventional wisdom in the first part of the twentieth century was that the universe had always existed and would always exist. This "steady state" universe seemed to match up with what astronomers saw in the skies, and a belief in an eternal and infinite universe prompted Einstein to modify his theory of relativity to fit a steady state universe. When Hubble proved that the universe was, in fact, expanding, astronomers were initially reluctant to believe him because if the universe is expanding, it suggests that there was a time in the past when the universe was born—that is, a moment of creation. Over time, as the evidence for this grew, most astronomers came to accept that the universe began with a Big Bang. But they still wanted proof.

That proof came in 1965 when Arno Penzias and Robert Wilson, two scientists at Bell Laboratories, discovered some irregularities in their measurements of radio antenna noise. After carefully and laboriously eliminating every possible source of interference, they finally came to the conclusion that what accounted for these irregularities was microwave radiation coming from space. They then found that this microwave radiation existed in every direction they looked. Later, when scientists calculated the temperature of the microwave radiation (using the radiation curve previously discussed), they found that the universe was almost precisely the temperature predicted by the Big Bang theory. Penzias and Wilson's discovery proved that the universe had a birth date. Recent research estimates this birth date was about 13.7 billion years ago. (Penzias and Wilson were awarded the Nobel Prize in physics for their discovery of this cosmic microwave background radiation.)

Cosmic microwave background radiation (sometimes abbreviated CMB) has been extensively studied in the decades since its discovery, most famously by the Cosmic Background Explorer (COBE) and Wilson Microwave Anisotropy Probe (WMAP) satellites. These satellites have enabled scientists to map the skies in microwave wavelengths and compile astonishingly detailed information. COBE, for example, showed that the distribution of radiation wavelengths precisely matches an object with a temperature of a little more than 2.5°C (about 4.5°F) above absolute zero. In short, this is the average temperature of the space that makes up universe, which makes it, overall, a very cold place. While there are

Figure 6.2 Bell Telephone Laboratory scientists Robert Wilson and Arno Penzias, the 1978 Nobel Prize winners in physics, pose in front of the antenna that helped them discover cosmic microwave background radiation.

very small deviations (discussed later in this section), they're not enough to invalidate the Big Bang. COBE proved beyond doubt the reality of the Big Bang to anyone who might still doubt its existence. The only remaining questions were what more information could be wrung from these data. It turns out there was a lot more to be learned.

One thing that the microwave "light" showed was that it was not completely even in all directions; it was very slightly hotter in one direction, and ever so slightly cooler on the other side of the sky. When astronomers took out everything that could possibly contribute to these irregularities, the differences persisted. In other words, the universe itself seemed to be hotter in one direction and cooler in the other. Nevertheless, the astronomers quickly realized that the universe itself *is* uniform. The temperature variation was caused by Earth's own motion through the cosmos itself, and this motion was causing the microwave photons to be slightly blue-shifted in one direction—the direction in which we are moving—and slightly red-shifted in the other direction. In other words, this remnant from the Big Bang tells us in which direction the Earth is moving across the universe. According to COBE, our local group of galaxies is traveling through the universe at a speed of between 372 to 403 miles (600 to 650 km) per second in relation to the cosmic microwave radiation.

An even closer look, using better data from COBE and the newer WMAP satellite, revealed something even more astounding: small fluctuations in the temperature of different patches of the sky, shown in images as small patches of different color (Figure 6.3). If the universe were completely homogeneous—if it looked exactly the same in every direction—this map would be incredibly boring because it would all be a single color. Furthermore, if the universe were completely homogeneous, we would probably not even be here to make these maps. In fact, we owe our existence to the fact that the earliest universe was just a little lumpy. These lumps had enough extra gravity to pull more material onto them, which gave them a little more gravity, and caused even more material to fall on them. With time, these lumps grew to become galaxies, stars, and planets. These maps show us that, even at the very earliest times, the universe had some

Figure 6.3 This WMAP image shows a full-sky temperature map of the cosmic microwave background anisotropy (directionally dependent, as opposed to isotropy) and foreground signal from our galaxy (in red).

Helioseismology: Probing the Sun and Other Stars with Sound

The earthquake that set off the 2004 Indian Ocean tsunami made the Earth ring like a bell. Seismic waves were detected all over the world, after passing through the crust, the mantel, and both inner and outer cores. Studying these waves—where they were detected, when they arrived, and their strength—continues to help geologists understand the inner workings of the Earth. Yet, the Earth is not the only object that will ring like a bell from pressure waves. These waves can also be used to probe the interior of the Sun.

When pressure waves pass through the Sun, they cause the Sun to vibrate a little and the star's surface to flex in and out when they rise from below. This motion can be observed through the Sun's spectrum: Even a slight motion will cause a measurable blue-shift when the surface is flexing out and a red-shift when it flexes inward. Seeing which parts of the surface are moving in which direction, how big those areas are, and how rapidly they are moving can tell a solar astronomer something about the inner

structure. From the start, the universe was destined to form the sky that astronomers see today. The dots of color on the WMAP picture of the sky represent the forces that, in the course of 13.7 billion years, gave rise to our galaxy, our star, and our planet.

The Big Bang was an unimaginably violent event. The early universe was hot and dense, and reverberations from the Big Bang made the entire universe, quite literally, ring like a bell. Bells, like any vibrating objects, can sustain standing waves. This is what produces the sound and what lets the ringing sound go on for many seconds after a bell is struck. The universe itself "rang" in a similar manner when it was still young, hot, and dense. And, like any standing wave, there were places where there was more motion than in structure of the Sun. Helioseismology—the name of this field of study—has shown, for example, that there are "jet streams" of gas circling the Sun, thousands of miles beneath the surface. It has also revealed sunspots forming on the far side of the Sun weeks before they rotate into view. In the short time it's been in use, helioseismology has revealed a tremendous amount about how the Sun is put together and how it works.

As it turns out, all stars vibrate. By measuring the spectra of other stars, scientists can see the effects of pressure waves running through them as well. Although astronomers can't see other stars in nearly the detail that they see our own Sun, they can obtain enough information to begin to get an idea as to how these stars are structured. One thing they have learned thus far is that our current computer models of stellar structure are fairly accurate. But it's a pretty good guess that, as tools become more sophisticated and provide more sophisticated information, it'll probably turn out that these models aren't quite as good as they originally seemed. And that means there's always more to learn about our universe.

others—more matter was likely to collect in places moving more slowly than in places with high velocities. These places formed the seeds of the universe around us and this is part of the reason that WMAP found the lumps it did. The universe is lumpy today, in part, because of the acoustics it had shortly after it first formed. We owe our existence, in part, to the acoustics of the universe when it was so incredibly young.

Amazingly, the microwave photons we collect today tell us that the acoustics of the earliest universe set the stage for the structure of today's universe—and the fact that we are here to see these things and to ask these questions. There can be no more fitting way to bring this book about light and sound to a close.

Glossary

acoustics   The science of sound

amplitude   The height of a peak in a wave

barometer   A device that measures atmospheric pressure

black hole   A region of space with gravity that is so strong that not even light can escape

cochlea   A snail-shaped structure in the inner ear where sound vibrations are converted into electrical signals that travel to the brain

cone   A kind of cell, located in the retina, that detects color

cornea   The clear protective covering on the outer part of the eye

crest   The peak of a wave

de-excitation   The release of energy from an object, such as an atom or electron, so that it goes from a higher energy level to a lower energy level

diffract   Spreading out or bending a wave when it encounters a small barrier or obstacle

Doppler effect   The shift in frequency that is observed in a wave when an object radiating that wave moves toward or away from the observer

electromagnetic wave   A kind of wave—including everything from radio waves to light waves to gamma rays—that carries electric and magnetic fields and can exist even in empty space

excitation   The act of adding energy to an object, such as an atom or electron, so that it moves from a lower energy level to a higher energy level

fluorescence   The light that is released when energized atoms or molecules give off radiation

focus   The location at which light waves from a point on a distant object join together, or converge

frequency   The number of wave crests (or troughs) that pass through a given point each second

gamma ray bursts   Powerful flashes of high-energy light in the cosmos, some of which may be caused by stars collapsing into black holes

helioseismology   The study of vibrations and sound waves on the Sun in order to learn more about what is happening inside and outside of it

hydrophones   Underwater microphones

incandescence   The production of light from a heated object such as a wire filament in a light bulb

infrasound   Sound that is too low-pitched for humans to hear

ionization   The process of adding enough energy to an electron so that it can escape from the atom or molecule that it is orbiting

iris   A small opening through which light enters the eye

larynx   The part of the throat that contains the vocal folds and is involved in producing the voice

laser (Light Amplification by the Stimulated Emission of Radiation)   A device that produces a narrow, intense beam of light having a single color

lens   An object that bends multiple incoming light rays so that they either move closer together or spread out

LED (light-emitting diode)   An electronic component made of a solid semiconductor material that gives off light when electric current passes through it

light   The region of the electromagnetic spectrum that contains the colors—from red to violet—visible to the human eye; the term is also sometimes used to refer to the entire electromagnetic spectrum, from radio waves to gamma waves.

longitudinal wave   A type of wave that moves parallel to the direction of the vibrations in a wave; a sound wave is a type of longitudinal wave.

medium   A substance such as air or water that a wave passes through

optic nerve   The fibers that transfer visual information from the retina to the brain

periodic phenomenon   Anything that regularly repeats the same pattern over and over again

phase   A property of a wave, describing the location of the crests and troughs of a wave relative to their starting point

photoelectric effect   A process in which light or other electromagnetic radiation ejects electrons from a material; it shows that light can behave as point-like particles.

photons   Particles of light

quasars (quasi-stellar radio source)   Very bright objects that lie in the center of certain galaxies

refraction   The bending or change in the direction of a light wave when it changes its speed as it moves from one medium to another

retina   The part of the eye that detects an image, transforms it into electrical signals, and shoots the information off to the brain

rod   The kind of cell, located in the retina, that can detect low levels of light but not color

sonoluminescence   The conversion of sound waves into light

sound   Pressure waves that move through a medium, such as air or water, causing atoms or molecules to vibrate back and forth, to produce auditory signals that can be heard

spectrum   The range of colors (wavelengths) given off by the Sun or any other object that releases electromagnetic radiation

standing wave   A kind of wave whose crests and troughs stay in place, instead of moving through space

telescopes   Devices that can see faraway objects such as planets, stars, or galaxies, by collecting light from distant objects and focusing it

transducer   A device that converts one form of energy (such as sound) into another (such as electricity)

transverse wave   A wave that moves in a direction perpendicular to the up-and-down motion of the wave's crests and troughs; a wave moving down a rope is an example of a transverse wave.

traveling waves   A kind of wave whose crests and troughs move through space

trough   The low part of a wave

ultrasound   Sound that is too high-pitched for humans to hear

vacuum   Empty space

vocal folds   Small flaps of tissue inside the larynx devoted to producing sound; they are commonly known as vocal cords.

wavelength   The distance between two peaks, or two troughs, in a wave

Bibliography

Boslough, John and John Mather. *The Very First Light: The True Inside Story of the Scientific Journey Back to the Dawn of the Universe*. New York: Basic Books, 2008.

Chaplin, William J. *The Music of the Sun: The Story of Helioseismology*. Oxford, England: Oneworld Publications, 2006.

Halliday, David, Robert Resnick, and Jearl Walker. *Fundamentals of Physics*. New York: Wiley, 2004.

Perkowitz, Sidney. *Empire of Light: A History of Discovery in Science and Art*. Washington, D.C.: Joseph Henry Press, 2008.

Rossing, Thomas D., Richard F. Moore, and Paul A. Wheeler, *The Science of Sound (3rd Edition)*. Upper Saddle River, NJ: Addison Wesley, 2001.

Singh, Simon. *Big Bang: The Origin of the Universe*. London: Fourth Estate, 2005.

Further Resources

Cerullo, Mary M. *Dolphins: What They Can Teach Us*. New York: Scholastic, 2000.

Despezio, Michael. *Awesome Experiments in Light & Sound*. New York: Sterling, 2006.

Hakim, Joy. *The Story of Science: Einstein Adds a New Dimension*. Washington, D.C.: Smithsonian Books, 2007.

Ouellette, Jennifer. *Black Bodies and Quantum Cats: Tales from the Annals of Physics*. New York: Penguin, 2005.

Oxlade, Chris and Corinne Stockley. *The World of the Microscope*. London: Usborne Books, 2008.

Parsons, Jayne, editor. *The Way Science Works*. New York: DK Children, 2002.

Web Sites

Acoustics.org
http://www.acoustics.org
> *This site provides information on the science of sound, including an online pressroom with some of the latest news in topics ranging from marine mammal sonar to ultrasound in medicine.*

Discovering Light
http://library.thinkquest.org/27356/index.htm
> *Read an introduction to the science of light, and find information about the use of light in technology, nature, and culture.*

Electromagnetic Spectrum
http://imagine.gsfc.nasa.gov/docs/science/know_l1/emspectrum.html
> *View descriptions and illustrations of the electromagnetic spectrum, from gamma rays and X-rays to visible light and radio waves.*

Exploring the Science of Light

http://www.opticsforkids.org/

>   *Explore activities, optical illusions, definitions, timeline, and biographies on optics for young people.*

Physics and Acoustics of Baseball and Softball Bats

http://www.kettering.edu/~drussell/bats.html

>   *Sports fans will be interested in this site's pictures, animations, and questions and answers about the sounds and forces involved when a ball meets a bat.*

Science, Optics & You

http://micro.magnet.fsu.edu/optics/

>   *This site offers activities and answers to questions about light, color, and optics.*

Picture Credits

Index

About the Authors

P. Andrew Karam is a scientist, writer and educator who has devoted himself since 1981 to radiation safety. He received his Ph.D. in environmental sciences from Ohio State University. He has written more than 100 technical articles and editorials in scientific and technical journals and newsletters. Karam has also authored more than 200 encyclopedia articles and several books, including *Rig Ship for Ultra Quiet*, which describes his first encounters with radiation science as a Navy technician on nuclear submarines.

Ben P. Stein has been a professional science writer since 1992. He earned his bachelor's degree in physics with honors at the State University of New York at Binghamton. He then attended journalism school at New York University, where he embarked upon a career in science writing. He worked at the American Institute of Physics for 16 years. Stein's writing has appeared in *Encyclopedia Britannica*, *Popular Science*, *New Scientist*, *Salon*, and many other publications. He lives in Columbia, Maryland.